MY HEARTFELT PASSION

Saving Our Nation One Child at a Time

Copyright © 2017 by Jim Davidson
All rights reserved

No part of this book may be reproduced or transmitted in any form or by any means, graphics, electronic, or mechanical, including photocopying, recording, taping, or by any information storage retrieval system, without the permission, in writing, of the publisher. For more information, send an email to support@sbpra.net, Attention Subsidiary Rights Department.

Strategic Book Publishing and Rights Co., LLC
USA | Singapore

For information about special discounts or bulk purchases, please contact Strategic Book Publishing and Rights Co. Special Sales, at bookorder@sbpra.net.

ISBN: 978-1-946540-25-6

Book Design: Jennifer M Rawls, Graphic Designer

MY HEARTFELT PASSION

Saving Our Nation One Child at a Time

By Jim Davidson

Strategic Book Publishing and Rights Co.

Dedication

Janis Davidson

This book is dedicated to my wife Janis who loves me, inspires me, stands by my side and is the greatest helpmate any man could ever have.

Table of Contents

Foreword 7

Introduction 11

1   The Powerful Hand of Fate 19

2   Turned on to Knowledge 33

3   The Daily Radio Program 45

4   Building a Good Vocabulary 55

5   The Weekly Newspaper Column 63

6   Challenged by a Friend 71

7   Hail to the Chief 81

8   The Conway Bookcase Project 89

9   The Annual Awards Ceremony 105

10 The Bookcase Fundraising Banquet 123

11 The American Profile Stops By 147

12 A Call to Action 157

Foreword

The year was 1921. The place was Mount Moriah, Arkansas. The event was the birth of a little girl.

She was born to a mother who loved her and a father who never understood his responsibilities as a father. He abandoned the family at the beginning of the Great Depression and never came back. Her mother worked odd jobs, took in laundry, and did whatever she could to squeak by. But they were poor – very poor.

The little girl's family was impoverished in a way that most cannot imagine. She never owned her own shoes until the seventh grade. The family sometimes only ate a single watermelon from the fields outside Hope that her brothers received as wages for picking melons all day long.

Not once did she eat lunch at school because she could not afford the school lunch and there was no food at home to bring. She was poor.

But her mother could read.

The little girl attended school in Hope, Arkansas, and experienced academic success. She was the only one of five children in her family to graduate from high school. In fact, she was "skipped ahead" twice in her schooling and graduated early.

The little girl became academically successful and beat the odds in school. Somehow she found the resilience inside to persevere and make it.

She became a vociferous reader and collector of books. She worked at the Little Rock Public Library and served as the librarian for her church for fifty-two years. Yes, fifty-two years.

The little girl – because of her unending thirst for books and for reading – became one of the most well-read people in her circle. She could tell you something about virtually everything.

She married and had a family of her own – all of whom graduated high school, all of whom attended college, all of whom became successful in life.

I know her story because she was my Mom.

Mom clearly did not start with the greatest of advantages. In fact, she was highly disadvantaged. And yet she did well due in large part to her mother's ability to read and her mother's constant nudging her to finish high school.

Not everyone with disadvantaged circumstances can make it out of their poverty to succeed. But like my mother, those who do usually depend on their ability to read. Reading goes a long way to putting all of us on a path to a better life.

What a great advantage a child has who enters school knowing and understanding the written word, who has been in an environment where reading is emphasized, where books are present in the home, and where books are valued.

Jim Davidson's "Bookcase for Every Child" project does exactly that – gives kids in low-income families a centerpiece for reading – a bookshelf. That was something that I took for granted as a child because our home was full of books. Reading was a constant priority set by my mother.

What a great opportunity you have today to speak into the future of children about the importance of reading. Give them a bookcase. And give them books. Lots of books.

As you read Jim's story about the history of this important project, I hope you will keep in mind those students who might not have a single example of what you are currently holding in your hand and that you take for granted – a book.

I hope you will also keep in mind a little girl who hailed from Hope and who found her hope for an escape from poverty through books. Her name was Joye.

Dr. Greg Murry, Ed.D.
Superintendent of Schools
Conway, Arkansas

Introduction

As I begin to write the introduction for this book, the first thing I want to do is to place things in perspective. The members of our Conway Bookcase Project committee, as well as many people in our community, are just as passionate as I am about helping pre-school children from low-income families to develop good literacy skills.

Those who serve on our committee will be identified by name later in the book. But in the first several chapters, leading up to 2005 when we began our project, I want to tell you my story since this will truly tell you why I am so enthusiastic about starting it, and continue to be involved. As you read, keep in mind that anything I may have done, or honor I have received, is to the Glory of God. To be sure, without His help and inspiration none of this would have been possible. And now, as the late television comedian Jackie Gleason used to say, "Awaaaay we go."

As a professional speaker, one of the best letters of commendation I have ever received came in 2001 from Chris Shoemaker, Director of Public Relations for Bluefield College, in Bluefield, West Virginia. His letter said, in part, "When we booked you as our lecturer, we thought we were getting an intriguing speaker who could discuss the business of being a journalist. What we actually got was a wise Christian man who, while sharing his words of wisdom about the media, touched our hearts, made us laugh, and inspired us to be more than just a better journalist, but better people.

You advised us that doing our jobs 'and then some' will make us better employees. You showed us that 'being the best we can be' begins with a positive attitude. You helped us realize that the road to success in all facets of life starts by being a servant to others. And you encouraged us to remember the really important things in life that lead to true happiness."

Certainly I am grateful for Chris's kind words, but I suspect that you, like many other readers, will also be surprised at what you will find in this book. Let me say here from the very beginning that my "heartfelt" passion is literacy, the state of being literate, "being able to read and write." Now, I can truthfully say this has not always been true for me. As I look back over my life, at some point I became truly concerned about those who were "illiterate." Over time, that concern evolved into making a real "commitment" to doing something about the tremendous illiteracy problem we have in our nation.

Now, after almost 47 years of doing my best to help people achieve success in life, I have developed a deep passion for those in our society who really do not have a chance when it comes to achieving true and lasting success. This is usually because they are illiterate, or have minimal literacy skills. Here in my community of Conway, Arkansas, we have developed a terrific literacy project to help those who are at the greatest risk, pre-school children being reared in low-income families.

I invite you to take a journey with me that started

with my birth on May 1, 1938, and travel to the present time. I will acknowledge a number of good people who "held my ladder" and were there at critical times when my career choices were not clear. Over the years my life has truly been exciting because I have always had a positive attitude, an optimistic outlook on life, and a desire to see and bring out the best in other people. My heartfelt prayer is that you will "catch" my enthusiasm and, after reading what I share, will join with me to help improve the terrible illiteracy problem we have in America.

Improving literacy sounds simple, and it is for those of us who are literate. But it means much more for the 42 million adults in America who cannot read at level one, the fifth grade. But what is tragic is the vast majority of our citizens do not know that illiteracy is a major problem in our country, one that is not only costing us billions of dollars in lost productivity but is the root cause of much of the violence, crime and the "course" turn our society has taken in recent years. You know something is terribly wrong when something as simple as going to the mall now has a fear factor not present even a decade ago.

What I want to do here in the beginning is to make a very important statement about an issue, one that is negatively impacting every single American, and then to share the steps that we have taken here in my community to do something about it. Here is the statement: The root cause of much of the violence, murder, suicides, robbery, car jackings, drug addiction, alcoholism, welfare, poverty and wasted human potential is illiteracy. Since birds of a feather flock together, when illiterates who do not have a job hang out with others who are also unemployed, we all pay a huge price relative to the things I have just shared with you.

We have many so-called "experts" who talk about a myriad of issues that relate to the many people problems we have in our society; but here is the meat of the issue, the root cause is illiteracy. The reason this is not obvious to more people is because it involves such a small percentage of our population. However, we all know that it only takes one rotten apple to spoil the whole barrel, and it only takes a few criminals, less than one percent of our population, to wreak havoc in any community, large or small. We certainly have them in our community, and I bet you do as well in your community.

If you will go to the "Table of Contents" of this book and examine the titles for the 12 chapters in this book, you will see a natural progression that provides a stable foundation for my mission today. After discussing my childhood and early years, I will also discuss my work as an educational consultant with administrators, teachers and students, who have given me some real insights. During the decade of the 1970s, I spoke to more than 500 different school faculties, plus many other educational groups. I will also share the beginning of my daily radio program that made it necessary for me to do a lot of reading and research. At this point, in the decade of the 1980s, I was convinced of and understood even more the value and power of knowledge. Later, in 1995 when I began my weekly newspaper column, I became even more aware of our terrible literacy problem, and this began to seep into my subconscious mind. At this point it became painfully clear that those who were illiterate could not even read and benefit from my column. In 2005 we began a unique literacy project that we named, "The Conway Bookcase Project," and we targeted pre-school children who were being reared in low-income families. As previously stated, these are the people who are at the greatest risk to fail and not become a contributing member of our society. This need became even more pressing for me when I learned from a loyal newspaper reader that 61 percent of low-income families in our country have no books at all in their homes for their children to read.

Our terrific literacy project continues to this day. We are now in six states and can truly see the potential for this project to spread to other communities throughout the country, and help our nation regain the high standing we had in math, science and reading just 50 to 75 years ago.

Just like building any structure that will last requires a strong foundation, I will also talk with you about how our committee was formed and about having a community-wide book drive. I will also discuss how we raise the funds to build the bookcases by holding an annual Bookcase Banquet, then the process of how we go about actually building the bookcases. After they are built, we line up qualified speakers and dignitaries to hold an annual Awards Ceremony to present the bookcases, with a starter set of children's books. They say that "a picture is worth a thousand words," and we have included many photos, especially in the chapters about the bookcase banquet and awards ceremony.

My Heartfelt Passion

As I write this we are in our 13th year of building and giving 50 personalized bookcases each year to children who need help the most. Many will fall through the cracks if some person or group is not there to help them. We have the knowledge and experience necessary to begin and maintain a project in every community in America, and we can give you the do's and don'ts of starting a bookcase project that we have found to work best for us. Our project is copyrighted because we know from experience that when we are willing to settle for less than the best, that is what we will have. And we definitely want the very best for our children, our nation's greatest resource.

Illiteracy is a terrible problem but, believe me, we can do something about it, so our nation will be in better hands and be safer for future generations of Americans in the years to come.

"A society becomes great when old men and women plant trees whose shade they will never sit in."

Jim Davidson
Nationally Syndicated Columnist &
Founder, Bookcase for Every Child©

THE POWERFUL HAND OF FATE

CHAPTER ONE

THE POWERFUL HAND OF FATE

It has been said that we can choose our friends but we can't choose our relatives. As a human being, you, me and every other person who has ever been born is the confluence of a genetic pool that goes back thousands of years. We are each unique. No other human being who is living, or has ever lived, has the same DNA, fingerprints, or voice print. Yes, we are truly one of a kind. The irony of all this is that we had absolutely no choice as to the color of our skin, where we were born, the identity of our parents, or the social and economic conditions into which we were born. We just showed up with all the potential given to us as unique human beings who were created in the image of almighty God.

Now the question comes: "What are we going to do with all of this fantastic potential we have been given?" It is here that the powerful hand of fate enters the picture. The word "fate," according to the dictionary, is defined as "the power supposed to determine the outcome of events before they occur; destiny." Some people call this power "chance;" others call it "luck," but based on my understanding and beliefs, I choose to call it "the power or the hand of God."

No one knows for sure exactly when man first appeared on earth, so our history truly goes back for an indefinite period of time. As the earth was populated and indigenous groups appeared, clusters of people with a common ancestry began to live in communities, mostly for protection. As the populations increased, and boundaries established, they found it necessary to have some form of government to protect them from others, and also from themselves. This has evolved to where today we have more than 200 different countries in the world, and dozens of territories that are governed by one of these countries.

If you were born in the United States of America, or have even become a naturalized citizen, you can thank your lucky stars, because fate, or whatever you choose to call it, has definitely smiled on you. You are one of the most blessed human beings on earth. In a little over 240 years, our nation has become the envy of the rest of the world. Our standard of living is the highest in history, and even though we have problems there are thousands of people who line up each year to enter and live in our country. If you don't know, you may ask what makes this possible? To answer this question, it is necessary to give you a little bit of our history.

The land mass that became America was discovered in the late 1400s by Amerigo Vespucci, a Florentine navigator and explorer who played a prominent role in exploring the new world. This land was named for him, both North and South America. Moving forward a century or so, our history in the United States of America really began when citizens of the country of England, our mother country, oppressed by the British Crown sailed to our shores seeking freedom and religious liberty.

With a stopover in Holland, these English Separatists came to our shores on a ship named the Mayflower in 1620, landed at Plymouth Rock, now Massachusetts, to establish the Plymouth Colony. These people were still subjects of the British Crown until 1776, when the Declaration of Independence was signed by representatives from our original 13 colonies. This action resulted in the Revolutionary War with Great Britain.

The rag-tag troops of the colonies, led by Gen. George Washington, won our independence and shortly afterwards representatives from each colony adopted the Articles of Confederation, and later drafted the United States Constitution that was ratified in 1787. Citizen George Washington was later elected our first president. What has made our nation unique in all of world history is our constitutional form of government, called a democracy, where the people hold the power and elect leaders to represent us in three branches of government, the Executive, the Legislative and the Judicial.

When our citizens were allowed to own property and produce products to sell for a profit, this resulted in a unique economic system that we call the American Free Enterprise System. This has given more people more opportunities to achieve financial success and independence than any other nation in the history of mankind.

There are two key words that make it possible for you and me to plan, succeed and achieve our personal goals, Freedom and Opportunity. Over the years I have said many times, "Give me opportunity and then get out of my way." Now, let us go back to something I said earlier and you will understand why I have written this book and why it is so important for those of us who are literate to help those who are illiterate.

Earlier I talked about "fate" and the fact we have no choice as to the color of our skin, where we are born, the identity of our parents, or the social and economic conditions into which we were born. From this point forward I am going to tell you my story and how "fate" smiled on me by having good parents who loved me, who taught me right from wrong and other character values, and who had good genes to give me a strong, healthy body that would later take me anywhere I wanted to go.

What I want you to see very clearly is that fate smiles on some people and does not smile on others, even here in great prosperous America. Just consider my story, and probably yours too, compared to that of a young baby born in a low-income housing unit to a mother on crack cocaine with five other children, each with a different father, and how each child grows up in squalid conditions without even knowing who their father is. My chances to succeed are so much better than this child's, simply because "fate" smiled on me and blessed me more than I deserved. Neither of us had a choice the day we were born.

When I watch the news on television each evening and see the crime, murders, car jackings, purse snatchings, and all the rest, I know that "fate" did not smile on most of the people who are committing these heinous acts. In 2016, there were more than 750 murders in the city of Chicago alone.

I believe with all my heart that illiteracy is the root cause for much of this violence. It may be too late for most of this generation (but there are adult literacy programs which are helping many of them, too), but not for future generations, and I truly believe we can help them. Again, this is why I am writing this book. In the coming pages I will present what we have done here in my community, what we have learned in the process, and how working together with responsible like-minded citizens we all can make a difference across our great nation.

I was born in 1938 in the White County community of Bradford, Arkansas. My parents were good people who loved me. I was typical of the millions of children born in a small town, into a middle-class family. We had warm clothes and plenty to eat, but not a lot of money to spend on things that were not necessities. My father was considerably older than my mother and was reared at Cuba, a community in Eastern Kentucky near the town of Mayfield. He told me in later years that he left Kentucky in 1919, running from the Grand Jury for shooting craps on Sunday. I am not sure whether he was telling the truth or not, but I suspect he was.

When I was about 5 years old my family moved to the Southeast Arkansas town of Gould in Lincoln County.

My Heartfelt Passion

My father had lived there for several years before he met my mother. For a while we lived out in the country from Gould. I remember when I was about 6 or 7 years of age, times were hard for us. A family by the name of Craig took us in, and we lived with them for several months in two rooms of their home. Over time, things improved and my parents began to operate a small restaurant as a way to earn a living. The kids in our town called it the "Greasy Spoon" and some of them said it "was the only restaurant in the state that was so bad the flies tried to get out." In school I was an average student, but like so many others had a lot of potential if I only applied myself. To tell it like it is, I was in the half of the class that made the top half possible.

My main interest in school was girls and sports, in that order, and I was a pretty fair basketball player, averaging 18 points a game my senior year. Something happened during my senior year that impacted the rest of my life. After a game in which I had a very poor performance, a local businessman, who was also on the school board, made some very disparaging comments about me. Like most mothers would do, when she heard about it my mother went to confront him. After a bit he said, "Well, I don't care anything about Jim Davidson." When I heard this, it stuck in my craw and that feeling lasted for many years. At the time I said to myself, "I will show him." And even though he has been dead for a long time, with God's help and the help of many friends, I believe I have.

While it took a lot of 10-cent hamburgers from our restaurant to pay the $60-per-semester tuition, the year following my high school graduation I went to Arkansas A&M College in Monticello. I had the full intention of playing basketball and becoming a coach. It was here that reality began to set in. My basketball skills were not sufficient to even make the team, much less setting the conference on fire. I really liked Zoology and Biology and made good grades. I even thought about becoming a doctor. While I did well in these two classes, the fact that I did not do well in math and could not even pass high school algebra, I could see the handwriting on the wall.

The following year, with only 50 hours of college credit, I dropped out of college and made my way to Little Rock, our state's capital city, where I had grandparents and other family members. After a short time I got a job at Arkansas Printing and Litho Company working in the warehouse taking paper to the machines in the plant. I started out at $1.35 per hour and worked hard, trying to learn as much as I could about my job and also the printing business. This would later serve me well because I also learned that all work experiences can be put to good use somewhere down the line.

After a few months I got promoted into the plant working in the bindery department and began to earn a little more money. I stayed with this job for seven years, but came to a parting of the ways for what I thought was a perfectly logical reason at the time, they wouldn't let me off to go deer hunting. That's a big deal in Arkansas, and was to me.

After deer season I began to look around for a new job. For me, this is where "fate" took over. I was blessed to be hired by Bert Parke, president of the Democrat Printing and Litho Company. He hired me as an outside salesman to sell printing to customers in the Little Rock area. It was here that my learning while working for my previous employer began to really pay off. I knew about the various kinds and sizes of paper, how the preparation was done, how printed jobs are bound and other important things that were of interest to my printing clientele.

After a few months I was doing really well financially, and Bert really took a liking to me. He was heavily involved in the community and began to encourage me to follow suit. Over the coming years I was named the Chairman of the Diamond Club, membership sales unit of the Little Rock Chamber of Commerce, served on the Pulaski County Quorum Court, was Chairman of the Speakers Bureau of the Pulaski County United Way, and was active in many other activities in the community as well as in my church. One thing for sure, Bert Parke "held my ladder" and before long I was to learn something that would forever change my life.

For many years, the Little Rock Chamber of Commerce had taken a Good Will Tour to visit other cities and to be hosted by the chamber in these cities. Bert, as the Co-Chairman of these tours, took me along. I went to San Antonio, Texas, the year the Hemisphere was opened; to Houston, where there were many highlights (especially a tour of the Astrodome); and to Denver, where we stayed in the Brown Palace Hotel, and even went snow skiing in Loveland, Colorado.

When I was growing up, my father talked with me many

times about honesty, treating others with respect, telling the truth and working hard to earn my wages. He also advised me to stay away from alcohol. He told me that before he had married my mother he had bought enough whiskey to float a battleship and all it did was keep him broke and the talk of the town. As a result, I have never taken a drink of alcohol of any kind, and while I have taken a few puffs, I have never bought a pack of cigarettes in my life. You can call it "luck" or "fate" or whatever, but that has been a real help to me.

It was during those chamber of commerce tours that I learned something that changed my life. Since I was not a drinker, I did not go out on the town and carouse with some of the other men. Rather I just sat in the hotel lobby, visited with several of the older men, listened to them and got to know them personally. Remember, these were the top community leaders in our state's capital city. What I learned is that the nicest, most helpful people are at the top and that I was very comfortable with them. When I got back home to my sales job, it was so easy to go to the top, talk with the "decision makers" and not waste time talking with people in the organization who could not make a decision. Later on, this would help me tremendously when I would stand before a large audience when I was retained to be their speaker.

Soon another event came along in 1968 that would also change my life. This is when I made the decision to take the Dale Carnegie Course. Bert Parke was so enthused about me taking the course that he paid for it. The course was fantastic, and the instructor was the late

Bob Gannaway. Bob was a wonderful teacher and a real Christian gentleman who helped me greatly. A part of each class in the 14-week course involved each member giving a one- to two-minute speech. To start this activity, Bob would call for a volunteer, and I would volunteer first every time until he finally caught on to what I was doing. My attitude was, if I am going to have to speak anyway, I may as well go ahead and get it over with. Besides, then I could relax while I listened to the other speeches.

I saw some of the class members so nervous they almost rubbed a hole in their pants before their time to speak. After Bob caught on to what I was doing, he made me wait until last to speak so the pressure would build on me, having to sit there. It must have impressed some of my classmates, because at the end of the course they voted me to be leader of the class and to get the personally engraved "Leadership Gavel." I still have it and treasure it greatly.

Well, things continued to go well with my printing sales, I was enjoying my community involvement, and a lot of blessings continued to come my way. Then one day I got a call from Bob Gannaway, who wanted to come by and visit with me. He invited me to go into business with him to distribute and sell the Earl Nightingale Motivation cassette tapes.

It was not an easy decision because I was now earning more than $25,000 a year selling printing, and that was a lot of money back then. However, I saw an opportunity to help other people who had a background similar to mine. Because it would involve a lot of public speaking, this was something I knew that I would love to do. So, in May of

1970 together we formed Motivation Services Inc. and opened offices in the Donaghey Building at Seventh and Main in downtown Little Rock. Bob was like a second father to me and definitely another person who "held my ladder." Do you have people like that in your life? Feel blessed if you do.

TURNED ON TO KNOWLEDGE

CHAPTER TWO

TURNED ON TO KNOWLEDGE

As I look back over my life, I can tell you that the decade of the 1970s was the most gratifying, in many ways, of my entire life. I had another one of those life-altering events happen to me. I had just left a financially rewarding printing sales job to start a business with my former Dale Carnegie teacher, the late Bob Gannaway, to distribute the Earl Nightingale attitude motivation tapes. These cassette tapes contained motivational and inspirational recordings. This was back in the days before the 8-track and CDs had come along. The beauty of cassette tapes was that people would play them in their cars while going to and from work, as well as on traveling between clients. These tapes became an "education-on-wheels" to thousands of people who wanted to get ahead.

In case you are not familiar with the late Earl Nightingale, here is a little background information. Earl was best known for his five-minute daily radio program titled, "Our Changing World." At one time it was carried by more than 1,000 stations, making it the largest commercially sponsored radio program in the history of broadcasting. Most of his sponsors were banks and savings and loans institutions. Earl had a rare voice that was instantly recognizable, and the content of his radio programs was a distillation of the wisdom of the ages from some of the greatest thinkers and writers of all time. He had accumulated this treasure from a lifetime of reading. (There we are back to reading again.)

He was also one of the few survivors of the battleship Arizona, which sunk when the Japanese attacked Pearl Harbor at the beginning of World War II. Later, he would rewrite and record much of the information from his radio program to form a series of motivational messages. An individual could listen to these and be both educated and inspired. Any salesman knows there are days when you are down and need a shot in the arm to get you going again.

The twelve-tape series that I loved most was titled "Lead the Field." He also wrote and recorded "The Strangest Secret," an inspirational message that became the only one in history to sell a million copies. That strangest secret is, "We become what we think about" and to be sure, this is worth thinking about. He became known as the "Dean of Personal Motivation." While Earl has been gone since 1989, his material can still be purchased from the Nightingale-Conant Corporation, based in Chicago. Just Google it and you will find it there.

This gives you a little insight as to what Bob and I were setting out to do. We wanted, first of all, to be of service to our fellow man, and in the process earn a good living. If you took all the various tape series, plus the printed manuals, it added up to about a $600 package, not a bad cost for an individual, a company, or a school to learn valuable principles and ideas that were proven to help maintain positive attitudes. It has been said that it is your "Attitude" and not your "Aptitude" that will determine your "Altitude." As William James of Harvard University once said, "The greatest discovery of my generation is that human beings can alter their lives by altering their attitudes of mind." This is what we were trying to do.

When we first started our company, Bob called on prospects, mostly those who had previously signed up some of their employees to take the Dale Carnegie course. Certainly, I could have called on various companies who needed motivation as part of their training program, and I also could have advertised as a speaker and traveled around the state and nation giving speeches. However, I did not relish the idea of getting on an airplane and being gone much of the time. Again, almost by fate, I learned that our public schools were the best prospects of all for what I was selling. The "buzz" word for most educators back in the 1970s was "Attitude." They had recently discovered that attitude plays a large role in and is responsible for 85 percent of an individual's success, while skill and knowledge make up the balance. In addition, school administrators were also looking for someone who could inspire and motivate their teachers.

This was especially the case for their pre-school workshop at the beginning of the school year. Later, as I did a survey and counted up the schools where I had been, I was surprised to learn the number was in excess of 500 faculties, plus dozens of student bodies, commencements and various educational conferences. As I visited the various schools and talked with the superintendents about a wide range of educational topics, I also gained a lot of knowledge and insights into the needs and challenges faced by our schools. I also traveled out of state to speak to a number of other educator groups.

While I loved speaking to the various groups, my greatest satisfaction came from working with the kids. Soon after I started, it did not take me two shakes of a lamb's tail to learn that the vast majority of students had no idea at all as to what they wanted to do with their lives. As a result, over the next several months I wrote and published a little 24-page booklet titled "How to Plan Your Life." This is actually a workbook, with fill-in-the-blanks, that I could spend time with a class of students and have them develop their own Life Plan.

The format was quite simple, but very revealing. It contained an introduction, and laws and principles, plus a section to answer six very important questions: Who Am I? Where Am I? Is it Possible for Me? Where Do I Start? Now What? and Is That All There Is To It? The booklet concluded with a thorough discussion of the major areas of life: Spiritual, Family, Work or School, Income, Time Management, The Importance of Habits, The Importance of Communication, Change, Continuing Education, and concluding with a "Check List" on the inside back cover.

Over the next few years, I conducted more than 50 of these six-hour "How to Plan Your Life" seminars with different schools around the state. The first three hours I would work with freshmen (ninth grade), because they still had time to work harder in school to prepare for a career choice. The last three hours I would work with seniors (12th grade), as they were about to be faced with

Saving Our Nation One Child at a Time

"How to Plan Your Life" booklet used in 6 hour seminars conducted by the founder.

reality, and often a cold and cruel world come graduation time. Some students would go on to college to further their education, others to join the military service, and still others to get a job. What made their choices so difficult is that 50 years ago there were a limited number of choices. For boys: if not college, back to their parent's farm or place of business, the military, or find a job somewhere. For girls: teaching, nursing, secretarial or work with a local business, especially banks. Back in the 1970s, there were more than 50,000 career possibilities. Today I am sure it's even higher.

While I did not set out to become a writer, the bug or the desire to write had set in on me. While attending a motivational conference for Nightingale distributors in Chicago in 1979, I met a man by the name of Winston K. Pendleton. Win is gone now, but he was from Windermere, Florida, and had been one of the speakers on our program, along with many other nationally known speakers such as famous television newscaster Lowell Thomas and the late Dr. Ken McFarland. Win was also an author and had written several books, mostly published by Pelican Publishing Company in Gretna, Louisiana. Win and I just "hit it off" and I told him about revising my "How to Plan Your Life" booklet into a full-length book, and that it was ready to be published.

The following week Win was kind enough to take my manuscript and talk with Dr. Milburn Calhoun, president of Pelican Publishing Company, and recommend that they publish it. They did, and his company would later publish a revised edition of my original book that is still for sale and is listed in their catalog. This is a large publishing company, and if you have ever heard of the late Zig Ziglar and his million-seller book "See You At the Top," you may know they also published his book. Little did I know then that this was the beginning of the writing of several other books, a daily radio program, and a nationally syndicated newspaper column. I am so grateful for everything that has happened and I know that God has truly smiled on me. Call it luck, chance or fate, America is truly the land of opportunity.

But back to what I was saying about my work with our schools. One of the greatest blessings I have ever received was that I made many good friends along the way. One of these was the late J.D. Barnett, Superintendent of the Valley Springs Schools, near Harrison, in Boone County, Arkansas. J.D. bought materials from me, twice had me speak to his faculty, and later to the student body. One year I was also commencement speaker for Valley Springs. The highlight for me came when it was time for him to retire after 30-plus years as Superintendent. The custom for the Arkansas Association of Educational Administrators was to present a plaque to retiring superintendents at their annual convention each year. At this special event the retiring superintendent was given the privilege of deciding who they wanted to make the presentation. It was a big day for him, and I was thrilled when he invited me to do the honor before 600 of his peers at the Educational Administrators annual state convention in Little Rock.

We have 75 counties in our state, and I have been privileged to speak in 72 of them. Without even being aware of it at the time, here is what happened that changed my life. When I first got in the business, I had a cassette player installed in my car and I listened to the Earl Nightingale tapes over and over again. I heard the best "quotes, ideas, thoughts and concepts from the greatest minds, writers, leaders, poets and philosophers" from all of recorded history. Here is what was happening for me, without me even being aware of it.

There are three keys to learning. The first is repetition, the second is repetition, and you guessed it, the third is also repetition. By listening to these great messages over and over again, especially early in the morning when my mind was clear, for 50,000 miles each year, I was driving these great thoughts deeper and deeper into my subconscious mind.

These ideas, thoughts and concepts would be there, plus what I am going to share in the next chapter, as I would write radio programs, columns, books, and even research for speeches. More on this later. One simple thing I learned from this experience is that we don't spend a lot of time reading or listening unless we have a compelling reason to do so. This is why it is so important for high school students to determine, or have some good idea, of what they want to do after they graduate. Sadly, many students drop out of school and do not graduate. And even more tragic are the large numbers of kids coming from low-income families who have no books to read growing up. They drop out way too soon, mentally and physically, to even have a chance to be successful.

Based on what I have shared with you so far, you can see that at this point in my life I got turned on to knowledge, and what it has meant in my life, and hopefully in yours as well. While earlier I did not know these things, God knew. And while I believe we make many of our own breaks, this is also how "fate" works in our lives. From my perspective, the problem for too many people is that they do not discern the quality of information they are taking into their mind. The English historian George Trevelyan said, "Education has produced a vast population able to read but unable to distinguish what is worth reading." Just think about the junk many young people are putting into their minds today and I believe you will also see why we have such monumental problems. We can do better. That is my prayer.

As a result of listening to great information on cassettes, I also became an avid reader. This has opened up a whole new world to me. My personal library has grown from just a few dozen books to a great number of volumes of many of the best and most enlightening books ever written. If you are an avid reader, here is a list of some of the books in my library that I have read (and re-read) and can endorse and whole-heartedly recommend.

1. The Holy Bible
2. The Tipping Point – Malcolm Gladwell
3. Outliers – Malcolm Gladwell
4. A Game Plan for Life – Coach John Wooden
5. Gifted Hands – Dr. Ben Carson
6. Same Kind of Different as Me – Ron Hall
7. See You at the Top – Zig Ziglar
8. The Strong Willed Child – Dr. James Dobson
9. How to Win Friends and Influence People – Dale Carnegie
10. He Still Moves Stones – Max Lucado
11. John Adams – David McCullough
12. Words to Lift Your Spirits – Coach Dale Brown
13. Common Sense – Thomas Paine
14. People Who Live at the End of Dirt Roads – Lee Pitts
15. The Thread That Runs So True – Jesse Stuart
16. A Walk Across America – Peter Jenkins
17. The Greatest Salesman in the World – Og Mandino

18. Tough Times Don't Last but Tough People Do – Dr. Robert Schuler
19. Psycho Cybernetics – Dr. Maxwell Maltz
20. Seven Habits of Highly Effective People – Stephen R. Covey
21. None of These Diseases – Dr. S.I. McMillen
22. Granny Camp: How to Bond With Your Grandchildren – Anne Dierks
23. Un-Common – Tony Dungy
24. The Anti-Alzheimer's Prescription – Dr. Vincent Fortanasce
25. A Framework for Understanding Poverty – Ruby K. Payne, Ph.D.
26. Battle Ready Moms Raising Battle Ready Kids – Reba Bowman
27. Don't Make A Budget – Ken Robinson

In the next chapter titled, "The Daily Radio Program," I will feature some of my highlights of the decade of the 1980s and I believe you will see the wonderful way God has blessed me. It is truly an honor to share many of the ideas that I have learned over the past years, and my daily radio program has provided a great venue for me to do that. I am honored to tell you about this experience.

THE DAILY RADIO PROGRAM

CHAPTER THREE

THE DAILY RADIO PROGRAM

Sometimes it is uncanny the way things turn out in our lives. After working with our schools as a businessman consultant for almost a decade, I made a decision to begin a Monday-through-Friday daily radio program. The plan was for a total air time of five minutes each day, with an introduction, three minutes of content, the sponsor's commercial, and concluding by the announcer telling listeners where they could get a printed copy of the program. This gave the sponsor some feedback as to the popularity and response to the programs, and also provided some prospects for their products or services.

This was in 1980, and there is little question that my decision to begin this program was influenced by the great success of Earl Nightingale's program, "Our Changing World." This is what motivated me, and proves the point that we truly do motivate each other. My work with our schools had convinced me that most young people have no idea as to a career choice, and what they want to do with their lives.

This was consistent with what I had learned while working with the Nightingale people that only five percent of all working people have clear, written goals, and can tell you what they are working to achieve, other than just having a job to earn a living. This is the primary reason I decided to name my radio program, "How to Plan Your Life." At this point in my life, I was also armed with the information I had gleaned from listening to those cassettes while driving 50,000 miles each year calling on schools.

Before getting a couple of months of programs written and ready to record, I had set up a recording studio in a small portable building adjacent to our home in North Pulaski County, Arkansas. However, there was one major problem for which I had not planned, my recording studio was on the flight path for airplanes taking off from Little Rock Air Force Base, headed west. At a very low altitude they came right over the top of my studio. To work around this problem I had to get up and record at 2 a.m. each morning.

I started narrating a program, and then heard the planes revving up their engines on the runway. I knew I could not finish before they came over, and the recording needle would pick up us competing with each other. The planes always won.

After a few days I was able to get some programs recorded and began the process of making sales calls to radio stations and potential sponsors to get my program on the air. If we are going to succeed in almost anything, we have to use the talents and skills with which God has blessed us, and in this respect I was very fortunate. In 1974, I was named the Arkansas Salesman of the Year by the

Purchasing Management Association, so it was easy for me to make contacts with good prospects. The first station to carry my "How to Plan Your Life" program was KARN in Little Rock, and my first sponsor was Griffin-Leggett Funeral Home. The owner of this funeral home was Harry Leggett Jr., who had become my good friend when I was in the printing business. Here was another example of how building good relationships pays off over and over.

I soon learned that funeral homes are marketing their services, that we are all prospects, that selling pre-need and pre-planning are important, and that my radio program was a perfect match for them. Later, I would also have banks and other types of businesses sponsor the program. The challenge to record my programs went on for several months, until one day I decided I had had enough and knew I had to move if I wanted to continue the program. I had relatives in the nearby Conway area and a favorite aunt who lived on Lake Conway. We both liked to fish, so I bought a lot in nearby Mayflower and we set out to build a home with a sound-proof recording studio. While this was happening, I continued to make sales calls in person or by telephone, and the number of stations running my program continued to grow.

On Feb. 26, 1984, another major milestone happened in my life that will chart my course for the remainder of my days. The church has always been important to me and I thought I was a Christian. But I came to realize that I had been just playing church and really did not know Jesus as my personal Lord and Savior. As a result I had made many poor choices and knew my life was headed in the wrong direction. On this date I walked the aisle in the First Baptist Church in Mayflower, accepted the Lord and was baptized a week later. Soon I was invited to teach a junior high boys' Sunday School class.

I accepted the challenge, but it did not take long for me to realize that I did not really know the Bible. At that point I made another important decision, to read the Bible all the way through in a year. The following year I continued, and this went on year after year until I had read it all the way through for 25 straight years. Of course, the process of repetition again took over and it was deeply imbedded in my subconscious mind. Now, every choice or decision I make is filtered and influenced by God's word. It was at this time that I truly began to understand what I had said earlier about "Fate" being the power or the hand of God. This became very clear when I read Proverbs 3:5-6 which says, "Trust in the Lord with all thine heart; and lean not unto thine own understanding but in all thy ways acknowledge Him, and He shall direct thy paths."

This has been a tremendous blessing to me, and I had no idea of the great things He had in store for me. Now I am more committed to the Lord and His church than ever before and He has given me peace that passes all understanding. The most important thing is that I do my best to live for Him day by day. It says in Psalms 119:11, "Thy word have I hid in mine heart, that I might not sin against thee."

Back to my radio show. Little did I know the challenge I would face in just a few short months. During a marathon recording session later in 1984, I felt a funny sensation in my throat and soon came to realize that I had a problem, I could not speak above a whisper. My problem was later diagnosed as a rare vocal disorder called Spasmodic Dysphonia, and it causes the vocal folds to lock-up and you lose your normal voice function. I was told later this condition often happens to preachers, singers, announcers and others who use their voice for sustained periods of time.

You can just imagine the anxiety I felt, as I had been earning my living speaking and recording radio programs. Before this happened, my voice was so strong that I could stand in the middle of a gym floor and speak to a thousand students without the aid of a microphone and be clearly heard by everyone in attendance. Needless to say, I was distraught. But God heard my plea, and like the story of Aaron and Moses in the Bible, He sent a man along by the name of Dave McCree who was a professional broadcaster. I don't remember how it all came about, but I had known Dave for several years and I assume he heard about my problem and contacted me.

At this point we worked out an arrangement for me to write the radio shows and he would come to my studio and record them. To his advantage, I just gave him a percentage of the sales, and even though he has not recorded any programs for me in several years, he gets a check from me each month that comes from the stations that still carry the program. As to my voice problem, I learned about a relatively new medical surgery procedure that could correct the problem. Dr. Bob McGrew, an Ear, Nose & Throat specialist in Little Rock performed this surgery for me. This operation is actually very complicated, but Dr. McGrew performed it, and in a few weeks I was on the road to recovery.

For almost a year following the surgery my voice had a very high pitch, but then it came back to a normal range. With the aid of a good microphone, I was back in business, at least to where I could have conversations and make speeches. Dave McCree was doing such a great job of narrating my radio show that I just had him continue. His voice was much better than mine and I am sure this is the reason our program was so well received and has stayed on several stations and their sponsors for more than 25 years. The sponsors pay the bills for the air time and my talent fee.

Earlier in this experience I claimed a special verse of scripture as my favorite verse. Romans 8:28 states, "And we know that all things work together for good to them that love God, to them who are the called according to his purpose." After my voice problem was corrected, I continued to make sales calls and secure new sponsors for the program. From my personal perspective, many people really do not understand what it takes to succeed or they are not willing to pay the price for success. Of course, as a small company, I did not have an expense account. I was the expense account.

Any successful small business person knows that you must hold your expenses down or you will soon be out of business. Back in the early days I had a pickup with a camper shell, and I outfitted it like a camper. I would stay overnight in some beautiful state parks, especially out of state. I could stay in a state park for about $9 a night, instead of a motel room for $50 to $75. Early in the morning I would shower, shave and get on my suit and tie, and then call on funeral homes and banks and talk with them about sponsoring my program. Most of them already had a business relationship with the local radio station. It took work, and some time, but I eventually had more than 300 radio stations, coast to coast, carry my "How to Plan

Your Life" program.

The greatest blessing I received from writing and producing the radio program was the hundreds of letters I received from our listeners. That was icing on the cake, to know that we were helping and encouraging people. After a decade of writing and having Dave McCree narrate my programs, in 1991 I was inspired to publish a book titled "You Can Be the Best", a collection of my favorite programs. Many listeners purchased it and were highly complementary of the selections we had made. This book was revised and reprinted in 1995, and after the third printing, I did not print again. Only a handful remain, but they are not for sale.

BUILDING A GOOD VOCABULARY

CHAPTER FOUR

BUILDING A GOOD VOCABULARY

One time I heard about an old printer who said, "I ain't never made but one grammatical mistake since I come to work here, I seen it when I done it so I taken it back." Obviously this old printer had a lot to learn, especially about the use of the King's English.

Would you believe there are more than 950,000 words in the New Webster's Unabridged Dictionary and the average American uses only 400 of these words 80 percent of the time in their everyday conversations? In this chapter I talk about the importance of building a good vocabulary, and why it is so vital to our success in life.

As an individual, there is one thing we cannot hide, except by silence, and that is the use of our language. When we open our mouth and begin to speak, we proclaim to the world where we are on the social pyramid, and to a large degree on the economic ladder of success. When I was with the Nightingale-Conant Corporation, I learned some things about our vocabulary as it relates to an individual's success that I have never read or heard anywhere else. Back in the early 1970s, Earl wrote of a 20-year study of college graduates that found, "Without a single exception, those who had scored highest on the vocabulary test given in college were in the top income group, while those who scored the lowest were in the bottom income group."

He also told about a study by scientist Johnson O'Connor, who gave vocabulary tests to executive and supervisory personnel in 39 large manufacturing companies. It found that, "Presidents and vice presidents averaged 236 out of a possible 272 points; managers averaged 168; superintendents 140; foremen 114; and floor bosses 86. In virtually every case, vocabulary correlated with executive level and income." Quoting Earl again, he said, "Let's face it, from the earliest times, the favored class of people has always been the educated class. They can make themselves recognized instantly, anywhere, by the simple expedient of speaking a few words. Our language, more than anything else, determines the extent of our knowledge."

In this regard, I have said many times that, "A person can go further faster, than any other way, if he or she can get on their feet and communicate their ideas forcefully and clearly to a large group of people." The truth is, no person can achieve real success without self-confidence, and taking the time to build a good vocabulary is one of the smartest ways to get it.

The real question then becomes, how do we go about building a powerful vocabulary? This is not something we can achieve overnight, but rather it takes time, and the slow and deliberate process of learning new words and what they mean, will make it happen. As we learn new words and what they mean, it becomes easier to work them into our normal conversations and also our speaking and writing.

Now, if you don't already know and believe these things, I hope you will allow this information to soak in, because it is also a big part of the solution to our nation's crime problem, which affects all of us. This is not to say that there are not college-educated people who commit crimes, because there are. But by and large, a person who is highly educated, especially if they have had some character training at home or elsewhere, is less likely to turn to a life of crime. It has been said, and rightly so, that our nation's greatest enemy is ignorance, and of course this is also true for the rest of the world. When we know enough of the right things, our lives will be much better and we will be happier and much more successful.

There are many ways to develop a good vocabulary, but a good place to begin is to keep a small dictionary handy each time we read, at least when we sit down to read an article or a good book. Just look up the definition of the words you encounter that you don't know what they mean. Also, set a goal to learn five new words each week and be able to define them, and you will be surprised at how quickly they add up and begin to make a difference in how you speak and write.

As a speaker, one thing I had to learn years ago was to know my audience and the basic level of education of its members. Several years ago I was the chairman of the Pulaski County United Way Speakers Bureau. It was my job many times during their annual fund-raising campaign, to talk with employee groups about giving to the United Way.

I recall one time speaking to all the management

personnel of one of our state's largest hospitals in their conference room. The next day I spoke to the dock workers at a large motor freight line, and they were assembled in a trailer that was hooked up to a truck that pulls an 18-wheeler. The value of every person, in the eyes of God, is the same but these two groups had different education levels, and this included a better vocabulary. So, it was important that I spoke their language as I made my appeal to them.

While very basic, it is still very important to understand that words are the tools that we use to communicate, regardless of the form it takes. When I was working with students in our schools, quite often I would ask, "What is the smallest unit of our alphabet? They would say "a letter." Then I would ask, if you put letters together, what do you have? They would say "A word." Then if you put words together, what do you have? They would say, "A sentence." Next, when you put sentences together, what do you have? They would say, "A paragraph." Now, here is where I was going. While it is true that we do have sentences, we don't teach students, at least some teachers don't, to look for the valuable and often life-changing ideas in the paragraphs.

It has been said millions of times that the world runs on good ideas. Please stop and think about this. Every single product or service that has ever been invented or developed to help mankind have a better life, started out as a good idea. And this idea was hatched from that small mass of gray matter that was lodged between the ears of some human being. The single greatest element to ever appear on earth is the human mind. One of the most wonderful things I have learned about the marvelous mind that God has given me, is when I have a problem all I have to do is give it to my mind and then watch it go to work.

It is often said that hindsight is 20/20, and this is so true. While I could not see it at the time, now as I look back over the course of my life, I can see the powerful hand of fate, or God, working with me and through me. As I listened to all those cassettes, read the Bible all the way through 25 times, and started a successful radio program, I did not realize I was building a pretty fair vocabulary at the same time. Of course, you do not have to be able to read to listen to the radio, but you do if you are going to write and produce a radio program. What I didn't know at the time, is the way God was preparing me to write a weekly newspaper column. It was during this time that my vocabulary really began to increase, but even here it was a slow process.

As we think about our nation and the future we will leave for our children and grandchildren, here is a thought by Martin Luther that is worth pondering, "The prosperity of a country depends not on the abundance of its revenues, or the strength of its fortifications, nor the beauty of its public buildings, but it consists in the number of its men of enlightenment and character." I am sure if Martin Luther were around today he would also include women, because they have made a tremendous contribution to the success of America.

THE WEEKLY NEWSPAPER COLUMN

CHAPTER FIVE

THE WEEKLY NEWSPAPER COLUMN

You may have heard the old saying, "Sticks and stones may break my bones but words can never hurt me." From my perspective, this is one of the biggest untruths ever told. Words are powerful and have the ability to completely destroy a human life, or they can soothe and lift us from the depths of despair and despondency and set our feet on solid rock. This is something I learned full well soon after beginning my weekly newspaper column. While I had some wonderful and positive comments from our radio listeners, it was nothing like the tremendous response that was to come later from my newspaper readers, when I began writing my weekly column and started putting words on paper.

The next several years and the start of the decade of the 1990s would prove to be very exciting. Due to the fact that we went to church in Conway, and did most of our shopping there, we made the decision to move to this very progressive and fast-growing community. After finding a great lot to build on south of town, we constructed a log home, with an office and recording studio. In this case, my past business experience really helped because I was able to incorporate a lot of good ideas into the plans that would serve our needs for many years to come.

After getting settled in, it was not long until a friend invited me to attend a meeting of the Conway Noon Lions Club. As you may know, the mission of the Lions is sight conservation and they have been doing it for over a century. In a few weeks I joined this wonderful group of people, and would stay for more than 20 years, serving in every leadership position and winning all their awards (including twice being named a Melvin Jones Fellow, the highest award in Lionism). I share all this because association with this group was significant in my career and service to my fellow man.

At one of our weekly meetings not too long after I joined the club, the speaker was Mike Hengel, publisher of the Log Cabin Democrat, our local daily newspaper. After the meeting I asked him if he would consider running something positive and uplifting for his readers each week. While we had never formally met, he knew about me because my "How to Plan Your Life" radio program had been running on our local radio station for several years. He said, "Let's take a look at it." That was more than 20 years ago, and little did I know at the time that his decision to begin my column would result in it being run each Friday, on the Opinion Page, and it is still running today. A few years later, another Log Cabin publisher, Scot Morrissey, made me an offer that has been very rewarding. He offered for the Log Cabin to design and host a website for my column in exchange for the paper running my column free of charge. It has worked out great and is still online. The address is www.jimdavidsoncolumn.com if you would like to check it out. It is password protected and entry is gained by newspapers that run my column.

When I first started writing the column in 1995, I used many of the ideas I had researched and developed for my radio program. Before long these ran out and the challenge to continually write and produce a weekly column was very rewarding and exciting. This forced me to use my mind, which was good and it helped me to improve my vocabulary. As I look back, almost from the beginning my policy was to write 13 columns at a time, because this lasts for a quarter and makes the billing and bookkeeping much easier. Since I had already developed a marketing plan for my radio show, it was just natural to follow suit with the column. One of the first things I did was to join our state press association as an associate member.

This decision provided me a new directory each year, giving a listing for important information for every newspaper in our state. In time I would secure a press directory for every state in the nation and develop a marketing plan to contact their newspaper members and ask them to consider carrying my column for their readers. During the period from 1995 to 2003, I had more than 375 newspapers in 35 states to run it. Some of these ran for just a few weeks, others for a few months, and still others for several years. I am pleased to say that a good number are still running my column today, even though I have not had the time to promote it like I used to. The newspaper industry has a formula to determine readership. At the pinnacle of my circulation, in the late 1990s, they told me, based on the number of newspapers and their subscribers, that I had more than a million readers each week. To this I can only say, "to God be the glory."

Not too long after starting my column, a reader, the late Mrs. Eva Easley in Bluefield, West Virginia, shared something that has impacted me greatly. She told me about a book titled, "Gifted Hands," by Dr. Ben Carson. I ordered this book and read it from cover to cover. His story goes back many years, way before he got involved in politics. Before his retirement, Dr. Carson was head of the Pediatric Neurosurgery Department of Johns Hopkins Hospital in Baltimore, Maryland. His claim to fame happened in 1987 when he, along with a team of doctors, performed the first-ever brain surgery where they separated Siamese twins conjoined at the head and both lived.

Ben Carson is an African-American who grew up with his brother Curtis in the inner-city of Detroit, Michigan. When he was very young, his mother, Sonya Carson, who had a third-grade education, divorced their father when she learned he actually had another family. Because of zoning, Ben and Curtis attended a mostly white school. In elementary school, Ben did not do well academically, and many of the other students called him "dummy." Before long, word of this "dummy business" got back to his mother. She had been working in the homes of many prominent families in the Detroit area, and had seen first-hand the importance and value of education. She did not waste any time and quickly took action. She demanded her boys read two books each week before they could go out and play. Needless to say they did not like her demand, but knowing the sacrifices she was making for them, they complied.

After a while of staying on this reading regimen,

Ben found that he loved to read, and his grades began to improve. They improved so much that before he left his former school, many of the white kids were coming to him asking for help with their homework. His academic success continued, and when he graduated from high school he was awarded a full four-year scholarship to Yale University. The rest is history, and his success was made possible because his mother cared enough to make him read. Wouldn't it be wonderful if all of America's children were so fortunate?

While his story did something special for Dr. Ben Carson, as a columnist it also did something for me. It helped me go from a general concern about illiteracy to something much more personal, a commitment to help children, especially from low-income families, have the advantage of books and being able to read. And not just read, but have a passion for reading, knowing they had a future much brighter than living in a ghetto that had mostly dead-end streets. Now, I know what the old bread man, the late television sportscaster Benny Craig meant when he said, "This is that old bread man with a bit of this and that from the world of sports, reminding you that no one ever stood as straight as the one who stoops to help a child."

As I write these words, I have researched and written more than 1,100 columns and I have a set of guidelines for writing that helps to encourage me, and to also keep me on track.

No. 1 – Pray before writing each one and ask the Lord to give me a clear mind and a specific purpose for what I want to accomplish for that particular column.

No. 2 – Columns should always be positive and upbeat, even for those with a negative topic.

No. 3 – Use humor when natural to do so, always being sensitive to any person or group when they are the butt end of the joke; use mostly self-deprecating humor.

No. 4 – Strive to always bring out the best in other people, and provide positive benefits for the reader.

No. 5 – Always strive to do the right thing and only use material that is consistent with high moral character, and do my best to be a good role model.

The hundreds of letters, phone calls and e-mails I have received from readers have brought the most satisfaction to me. One reader in Foley, Alabama, told me they read one of my columns each week to begin their Rotary meeting. Other readers tell me they have them on their refrigerator, others say they have a file or a box they keep them in, and some people read them in their Sunday school classes. There is one thing we all need in these tough times and that is encouragement. I try to do that through my column.

CHALLENGED BY A FRIEND

CHAPTER SIX

CHALLENGED BY A FRIEND

Carolyn Wilson

The powerful hand of fate and the love of God continued to move me forward to a special encounter with destiny. I will always be grateful they were there to have a tremendous influence in my life. In 2002 I became a Newspapers in Education (NIE) sponsor for our local daily newspaper. This is a nationwide program, coordinated by state press associations and member newspapers, in which companies and individuals pay for a set of newspapers that are delivered to a designated class in one or more local elementary schools.

A newspaper in the hands of a gifted teacher can be used to teach students, usually around the fourth grade, a multitude of useful, practical and valuable information that will benefit them for the rest of their lives. Of course, reading is paramount, which is the key to learning everything else (other than by observation), and students by this time should be reading at grade level. There are a plethora of reasons why studying newspapers in a classroom makes a real difference in the lives of students. According to research by the Newspaper Association of America Foundation, here are some of the many benefits.

1. Newspapers are an influential and integral part of our society. Freedom of the press is guaranteed under the Constitution.
2. Newspapers are more timely than textbooks. They are updated daily and keep students informed on current events.
3. Newspaper news stories are models of clear and concise writing. The newspaper also contains many different types of writing models: narrative, persuasive, expository. Newspaper stories are also written for various reading levels.
4. With the electronic newspaper, select pages can be printed and then marked, cut, pasted and colored – which makes it useful for young children even before they learn how to read. It's active not passive learning.
5. The newspaper is such a vast store of information. It contains something for everyone: science as it happens, real math problems, sequencing using comic strips. The list goes on and on.
6. Newspapers bridge the gap between the classroom and the "real" world. Students learn life skills, make career decisions, and become more motivated to learn by using the newspaper in the classroom.
7. Newspapers can stand alone as teaching tools, or be used as supplements to other instructional

materials such as the Internet.

8. The advantage of using the newspaper in the classroom is well-documented by research. A compilation of this research is available in "The Newspaper: A Reference Book for Teachers and Librarians." By Dr. Edward F. DeRoche, 1991.)

9. Newspapers in Education programs have a wealth of additional services to offer teachers, such as in-service workshops.

10. Participation in NIE is FREE to educators!

The classroom I sponsored was at the Ida Burns Elementary School here in Conway and the teacher was Kathy Sweere, who was the 2004 "Math Teacher of the Year" in Arkansas. My NIE students were in good hands. After several weeks of having the newspapers to study, Kathy invited me to come and speak to her class, and what a blessing it was. All the students were polite and eager to listen and to learn, and I consider my sponsorship a very good investment in their future. I encourage anyone who has the opportunity to get involved in the NIE program.

Then one day a few months later, I was talking with my friend Carolyn Wilson, then executive director of the Mississippi Press Association, and was telling her about my involvement with NIE. Before the end of our conversation, she said something that I took as a challenge, and that was for me to publish a book of my columns and give the profits to the NIE program. This was something so simple but yet had a profound effect on my future, and leading to my heartfelt passion for literacy. I will always be grateful to her. She has retired now, but is such a wonderful and efficient lady. I recall one time speaking to the annual

My Heartfelt Passion

banquet for the Yazoo City Chamber of Commerce, and she drove all the way from Jackson, Mississippi, to hear me.

As I thought about publishing a book of my columns, and what the title should be, I came up with "Learning, Earning & Giving Back", based on a very simple but important concept. The average life expectancy of Americans is now around 75 years, with women outliving men by several months. When you examine the title in view of this fact, the "Learning" could be the first 25 years during which most of our formal education takes place. The next 25 years could be the "Earning" years as we move out into the world to pursue a job or career to meet our financial needs. And finally the "Giving Back" years as we approach retirement and, if we have succeeded financially, have the time and money to give back to provide opportunity for future generations. The army of volunteers who "give back" is a major reason America has become so successful.

I followed through and did publish a book of my columns in 2003, and I have used it largely as Carolyn suggested.

Little did I know at the time but help was to come from a man who would become my good friend and one of those rare people I have talked about who "held my ladder." This man's name is Dr. Dennis Schick, who is also now retired but served as executive director for the Arkansas Press Association for more than 25 years. Dennis is not pretentious and never uses the term "Dr." in his speaking and writing, and most people who are around him do not know that he taught advertising and journalism at four major universities and has a line of credits a mile long.

I had gotten to know Dennis over the past few years as an Associate Member of the press association, especially in giving me ideas about self-syndicating my newspaper column. But when I shared with him the idea that Carolyn had presented to me, he offered his assistance. That was in 2003, and he has been helping me ever since. We have something in common in that we are both working harder now than when we were gainfully employed. Of course it's not really work if you have something to do that you truly enjoy. Dennis has a servant's heart, and he always has a ton of useful and helpful ideas.

At that point I had written about 350 columns, and Dennis contacted some of his "award winning" journalist friends and asked them to read all my columns and rate those they liked best to be included in the book. Of course, our mutual purpose was to support the NIE program. We all knew that helping these young children was in the best interest of all Americans. The names of each of those journalists are listed along with their photos in the back of the book.

What follows is a little information about each one at the time the book was published: DAVID R. BELL, A native Iowan who was publisher of the twice-weekly Leader-Union in Vandalia, Illinois. After college he worked in the national headquarters of the Fellowship of Christian Athletes in Kansas City. He has also served as president of the Illinois Press Association.

BYRON G. CRAWFORD – A featured columnist who was most at home on the Kentucky Page of the Louisville Courier Journal and his work has been featured in such newspapers as The New York Times, Los Angeles Times, USA Today and the London Sunday Telegraph.

JIM FALL – Executive director of the Montana Press Association in Helena. He spent his entire newspaper career working as a community journalist, first as a reporter, editor and publisher/owner of newspapers in Arkansas, Missouri and Illinois.

JIM HAMILTON – Managing editor of the Springfield Magazine and editor of the Buffalo Missouri Reflex newspaper for over 24 years. He is a past president of the Ozark Press Association, the Ozark Writers League, the Writers Hall of Fame, the Buffalo Area Chamber of Commerce, the Dallas County Fair and the Buffalo Kiwanis Club.

RAY LAAKANIEMI - Now lives in Kendallville, Indiana, after retiring from teaching journalism for 22 years at Bowling Green University. His book, "The Weekly Writers Handbook," is the best-selling instructional manual for weekly reporters and editors in the country.

C. DENNIS SCHICK – Retired after 25 years as executive director of the Arkansas Press Association. He came to APA from a 15-year teaching career at the University of Texas, Oklahoma State University, Southern Illinois University and the University of Illinois. He is the author of several books on advertising, graphic arts and political campaign strategy. He's also a Christian magician.

S. GRIFFIN SINGER – He directed the Dow Jones Newspaper Fund Copy Editing Center at the University of Texas and also helped create their Sports Journalism Program. He was in the newspaper and teaching businesses for over four decades.

RICHARD V. TUTTLE – For many years he served as executive editor of the News-Topic, a daily newspaper in Lenoir, North Carolina. Besides writing thousands of articles, editorials and columns for his own newspaper, for which he has received many awards, his pieces have appeared in the St. Petersburg (Florida) Times and the Weekly World News.

TIM L. WALTNER – He is the publisher of the Freeman Courier, a 2,000-circulation weekly in Southeastern South Dakota. He is a four-time winner of the Golden Dozen Award, given by the International Society of Newspaper Editors for editorial writing. He has served two terms as president of the South Dakota Newspaper Association.

Needless to say, I felt very honored to have these outstanding journalists read my columns and select those they felt worthy to be included in my book. Another highlight for my "Learning, Earning & Giving Back" book came when the advertising agency in Atlanta that represents Chick-fil-A contacted me about doing a column on one of the founder Truett Cathy's books. I was delighted to do it, because he is a wonderful gentleman and has such a long history of helping others, especially young people. While these discussions were taking place, I asked Mr. Cathy to write the foreword for my book and he accepted my invitation.

The book that I have been talking about, "Learning, Earning & Giving Back" contains 49 of my most requested columns and was published in 2003. It has continued to play an important role in fundraising for our bookcase literacy project, of which I will tell you more in detail in future chapters. Yes, passion is a wonderful thing if you are passionate about the right things. In the next chapter I will pay tribute to a man who inspired me to think outside the box. It is titled, "Hail to The Chief."

HAIL TO THE CHIEF

CHAPTER SEVEN

HAIL TO THE CHIEF

Chief Randall Aragon

When the President of the United States attends a formal ceremony, the familiar "Hail to The Chief" is played. Its lyrics are very beautiful and touching. He is the Commander In Chief for all our nation's military forces all over the world.

In this chapter I want to pay tribute to a man who was also a chief. In this case, it is my friend Randall Aragon, who was Chief of Police here in Conway, Arkansas, a few years ago. Randall inspired me to think outside the box and was very instrumental in starting the Conway Bookcase Project back in 2005, a couple of years after he came to our community.

I believe I may have the distinction of being the first person Randall met personally when he came to our city. When the chief's job came open, he was one of a great number who applied. At the time, he was Chief of Police in Lumberton, North Carolina. In view of Randall's upcoming interview with the selection committee, his wife had been reading my column online, and she told him, "You should get to know this man." One day shortly after that, I got a phone call from Randall telling me who he was and that he had applied to be our next police chief, and he wanted to take me to dinner the evening before his interview the next morning.

The following evening I picked him up at the motel where he was staying and we had dinner at a nice restaurant. I drove him around town and told him what little I knew about politics in our town and some of the challenges he would be facing. But mostly I gave him a birds-eye view of the great community that is one of the best places in America to live, work and rear a family. We are so proud of our three colleges, the business district and the downtown area, the many businesses in the area, and the surrounding scenery. I also showed him the building where the chief's office was located. It was a wonderful evening and I dropped him back off at his motel, and we parted company.

The next thing I knew, a few weeks later, is that Randall had gotten the job and was the new Conway Chief of Police. Quite naturally I was his friend, and it was nice to know the head of law enforcement in our community. After he and his wife got settled in, it was only natural that I invite him to attend a meeting of our local Lions Club, where I had been a member since 1995. Looking back, this was significant because it gave me the opportunity to see him on a regular basis and to really get to know him. All this time I continued to pursue my career writing and selling my newspaper column and making speeches in Arkansas and other cities around the country.

Some of the things I learned about Randall that would

soon have an impact on my life is that he grew up in Hell's Kitchen in New York City, and that his mother was an avid reader. He said quite often when he came home from school he would find her sitting in her favorite chair reading a book, and this influenced him to also become a reader. He went on to say that while he was in junior high school he constructed a bookcase out of metal rods and kept his books there. It was about this time that I heard from a reader in Bluefield, West Virginia, that only 61 percent of low-income families in America have any books at all for their children to read. Randall and I talked about this and we realized that if they had no books they sure did not have a place to keep them. Randall was unique in that he completely understood the link between illiteracy and crime.

One thing led to another, and I eventually asked a friend by the name of Howard Welch, who was a member of my Sunday school class and had a woodworking shop at his home to make us a sample bookcase. When he finished the case, it was beautiful. Any kid would be proud to own it. As time passed, we began to think about starting a bookcase project, with the plan to give a bookcase to each of the children in our local Head Start program. It just so happened that the director of the agency that included Head Start was Phyllis Fry, who was also a member of my church.

It was not long before Randall and I shared this idea with Mayor Tab Townsell, and he was excited as well. We took him to lunch a few days later to give him the details and what we had in mind. Our next step was to contact some of our local like-minded people who might want to be involved. Because my column had been running in our local daily newspaper for several years and Randall was still fairly new in town, I knew most of the people who would have an interest and be highly qualified to make a bookcase project successful. So it was only natural that I handpick most of the committee members. Looking back, I truly believe the reason our project has continued for so long, now in our 13th year, is because of the quality of people who were on our original committee.

It turns out that five of our original committee members were also fellow Lions, not because they were Lions but because of the positions they held in our community. In addition to Randall and myself, Lion Ken Ingram was an architect and he drew the plans for the bookcases; Lion Phyliss Fry, executive director of the Community Action Program for Central Arkansas/Head Start; and Lion Amanda Moore, head librarian at Hendrix College. Also serving on the committee were Scot Morrissey, Publisher of the Log Cabin Democrat; Mickey Cox, retired business executive and master craftsman; Nina Russ, housewife; Ruth Voss, Faulkner County Librarian; Dr. Larry Pillow, Pastor of Cornerstone Bible Church; Linda Linn, business woman; Nancy Mitchell, retired school teacher; Linda Hammontree, retired school counselor; and Mary Boyd, executive director of the Conway Housing Authority.

We had our first committee meeting on June 9, 2005, at the City Hall in Conway, and this turned out to be the first of only two committee meetings we ever had because we are all busy people and most all of the details of the project could be handled by group e-mail. Keep in mind that at this point we were flying by the seat of our pants because, to our knowledge, what we were undertaking from a community-wide effort had never been done before. We have learned so much in the past 13 years, and this is one of the primary reasons I decided to write this book. I want to pass along the benefit of our experiences and also what we learned that can be helpful to others.

In the following chapter I will tell you who we elected officers, the guidelines we established for the project, and how we were able to raise the money to buy the materials to build the bookcases. To be sure, Chief Randall Aragon was very much a part of this project for several years. He suggested and helped arrange our first awards ceremony, where we had television coverage from two major networks, and he also had me as a guest on his own Thin Blue Line television show. Later, he wrote an article about our project for the International Chiefs of Police magazine. However, a few years later he moved on to another Chief of Police position in Texas, and then on to Fairbanks, Alaska, where he has helped to establish a Bookcase for Every Child project. We will always be grateful to Randall for his contribution, which leads me to say again, "Hail to The Chief."

CHAPTER EIGHT

THE CONWAY BOOKCASE PROJECT

The famous children's author, Chinese-born American Katherine Paterson once said, "It is not enough to simply teach children to read: we have to give them something worth reading, something that will stretch their imaginations – something that will help them make sense of their own lives and encourage them to reach out towards people whose lives are quite different from their own."

There is no question that literacy and being able to read has the power to completely transform a person's life. On the other hand, those who never learn to read are left in the dark ages, and they live in a world where countless opportunities to have a happy, productive and successful life continue to pass them by. Understanding this is the motivation that stirred my soul and has caused me to have a heartfelt passion to make a difference in the lives and futures of underprivileged children.

It is always easier to look back and see where we have

been than it is to look ahead to the uncharted waters of the future. In this respect I definitely have the advantage, as I write these words to enhance the process of understanding. We are now in our 13th year since beginning the Conway Bookcase Project. In the previous chapter I listed our original committee members and the role they have played in our project.

At our first committee meeting we established some guidelines that would serve to anchor the project and to reinforce the fact that what we would always strive for is "sustainability." It would do little good to begin a project and then, in a few years, drop it and let it go by the wayside. If we are to improve literacy in our general population, it will take time and real staying power. This is why the character, integrity and commitment to excellence on the part of our members are vital for our long-term success.

One thing that distinguishes our project and sets it apart from all others is that we understand that illiteracy impacts every person in the community. This is the primary reason that having really good schools is a community's greatest asset. This results in better paying jobs and a standard of living that benefits everyone. We made the decision to name our project the Conway Bookcase Project. For other projects the name should be the same as your city or town, as in the DeKalb/Sycamore Bookcase Project, the Fairbanks Bookcase Project, the Bridgeport Bookcase Project, the Cleveland Bookcase Project, and so forth. This enables the entire community to get involved and improve literacy.

We never want to exclude anyone from being a part of our project, but over time we found that various groups like civic clubs, churches and even a city government,

Saving Our Nation One Child at a Time

wanted to start a bookcase project and put their name on it. This is not to say that they would not help some children, because they would. However, they would not do as much to improve literacy in the entire community as our plan does. This would be like cutting one small slice out of a whole pie and leaving the rest to spoil. For this reason, we copyrighted our project. There is room for a little flexibility but not for some other group to put their name on it. They should get involved and contribute to the whole community like everyone else.

What our committee decided at our first meeting:

1. We wanted our project to be all volunteer, with members "giving back' and no person would earn any money for their good work.

2. We wanted to target pre-school children being reared in low-income families. Statistics tell us these are the ones with the greatest risk of dropping out of school because they have few, if any, books in the home for the children to read.

3. Since the director of the Community Action Program for Central Arkansas (CAPCA) that includes Head Start was a member of our committee, we decided to work with their children, because federal guidelines mandate that for a child to be enrolled in Head Start, their parents must be low income.

4. We made the decision to build 50 bookcases each year, as this would cover most of the children

in our local Head Start program. Since we were all volunteers, the decision to build more than that would result in making it more difficult to secure craftsmen in future years to sustain the project.

5. The committee elected me, Jim Davidson, to serve as chairman of our project, and Amanda Moore to be secretary/treasurer of the Conway Bookcase Project.

6. Since our financial needs would be minimal, and since all the money we would need was just to buy the wood and supplies to build the bookcases, we elected not to be a 501 C-3 corporation. All that is needed to open a bank account is a committee member's Social Security number and to open the account as non-interest bearing, as this action would make it unnecessary to file a tax return.

7. As a final action of our committee, we agreed that since we were all so busy, group e-mail was the best way to communicate with each other. As chairman, I would keep everyone informed and issue a call to action when we needed to get things done. It has worked well, even to this day.

The beauty of having a community-wide literacy project like ours is that various committee members could be working on different parts of the project at the same time. The first thing we needed to do was to have a newspaper reporter, or a member of our committee, write a good article to be published in our local newspaper that would let our fellow citizens know about our unique project, state the need and goals, and ask them to help us. The second thing, with the help of all media outlets was to conduct a "book drive" to get the books needed to go in the bookshelves when we present them to our children.

Soon after we started our project we received over 6,000 children's books in less than three months from our local citizens. However, when we had our book drive, we failed to state that we only needed pre-school children's books. The excess of over the 3,000 books we needed was donated to the Boys & Girls Club, and they were put to good use. In future years we always stated that we need Pre-K books only, as this is in keeping with our philosophy that we target children with the greatest need.

Here committee members and others are sorting books to go in the bookcases to be given to Head Start children at our upcoming Awards Ceremony.

For years, many people across our nation, especially policy makers, have believed that having and spending a lot of money would help to solve our nation's illiteracy problem. It never has and never will. What we truly need is parents and others committed to reading and spending quality time with their children, and providing good books for them. This needs to begin almost from the cradle to foster a love of reading that will last a lifetime. As the twig is bent, so grows the tree.

It was here that I made an important decision regarding my daily newspaper column. For the past several years I had worked hard and saved a good deal of money. I had saved enough, combined with my monthly Social Security check and income from my radio program and newspaper column, that I would no longer market my column. I could not do justice to both them and the bookcase project. With the great need for the bookcase project, I just felt it was more important to spend the remainder of my days focusing on it.

But back to the project. It was now time to make plans to build the bookcases. The first step was to raise the money to buy the wood and supplies to build them. In addition to what was given at our first committee meeting, I sold copies of my "Learning, Earning & Giving Back" book, and donated all the proceeds. Then I went around the community and asked for donations from the Conway Corp. electric utility, Conway Regional Medical Center, and a number of banks. It did not take long until I had the $2,500 we needed to buy the materials. We did this for the first couple of years and then the Lord gave me a terrific fundraising idea. I will share this in another chapter.

Now, with money in hand, it was time to get started. As previously stated, there are craftsmen in every community who are retired or semi-retired who would be more than willing to help build the bookcases. Here in Conway I have known such a man for many years whose name is Mickey Cox, a retired executive from the Entergy Corp. Mickey is an excellent craftsmen and he builds beautiful furniture. When I asked him about helping to build the bookcases he said, "I will give it some thought." A few days later he came back to me with a terrific idea. He said, "We can use the plans Architect Ken Ingram has drawn to cut out all the parts, and then, after we build a set of five 'jigs,' use all glue, and produce them on an assembly line."

One of our volunteer craftsmen, Dale Wynkoop, is seen cutting out parts to build a bookcase. This is done outside to keep sawdust from harming the inside carpet.

Mickey recruited a crew of men from his church, Woodland Heights Baptist Church, to help build the bookcases. These men, Mickey Cox, Dale Wynkoop, Bill Clements, Richard Ogden, Wayne Gatling, Lynn Ward, Jim Capps, Jerry Nichols, Don Hood, Jerry Duncan, Gerald Charter, Mike Gober, Jim Wiedower, Dave Milligan and Don Hanson, got so efficient that they could produce eight

My Heartfelt Passion

to 10 bookcases each day. These men worked at different times, some longer than others, but they were all vital to the construction process. The best part about it is that it does not take long to build 50 bookcases, and this only takes place once each year.

Our personalized bookcases are handcrafted and held together by glue. This requires two glue-ups and the use of "jigs" that are held together by 2 x 2 board clamps.

After the bookcases were built, stained and varnished, a personal brass nameplate was added and the finished bookcases were probably the nicest piece of furniture in most of the children's homes. Also, a special word of thanks to David Bailey, owner of Bailey Painting Company, who provided his shop and equipment for our craftsmen to stain and varnish the bookcases, and to Tom and Kurt Meurer of Conway Trophy & Awards, who provided the nameplates free as their way of giving back.

Since we needed a place to build the bookcases and

to sort children's books, we found another friend and committee member, Dr. Larry Pillow, pastor of the Cornerstone Bible Church. He volunteered to let us use his Fellowship Hall to build the bookcases. Before the work actually started we put down some tarps to protect the carpet, and did all the cutting and sawing outside the building to keep the sawdust from being a problem. We also had some of our lady committee members sort the books to present with the bookcases when we had our first annual awards ceremony.

Every community in America has volunteer craftsmen who care about kids in low-income families. Many will gladly give their time and talents to build bookcases to help them.

This is how we continued to build the bookcases year by year. After a couple of years our men made the decision to move to the home woodworking shop of Bill Clements, also a great craftsman and a member of the Conway School Board. Then 11 years later, Mickey and most of his crew retired, but right on schedule the Lord sent us another great friend in the person of David Elms, who owns a cabinet shop, has a computerized saw to cut out the parts, and the employees to assemble them. When they finished building, we had a group of volunteers to come to his shop to help stain and varnish them. Later, when they dried, David had a couple of his employees install the nameplates.

At our Inaugural Bookcase Awards Ceremony we had all 50 bookcases lined up in the Fellowship Hall. What a sight to see parents and children looking for their very own.

Finished bookcases are seen here waiting to be loaded in a vehicle. Each one taken to a low-income family's home where a four-year old child's reading journey begins.

Saving Our Nation One Child at a Time

There have been many highlights over the years. A couple of years after we started our project, then-State Rep. Linda Tyler, a big supporter, invited us to have a press conference at the state Capitol. After the press conference, she took us to the House of Representatives while the members were in session. When the Speaker of the House introduced us, up in the gallery, the members gave us a standing ovation. What a thrill for all of us. We later had an opportunity to meet and visit with the governor and have our picture made with him in his conference room.

Strong supporter of our project, former State Representative Linda Tyler, seen here at our ceremony with Founder Jim Davidson.

Another important highlight was in 2010, when our project was given the Distinguished Service Award by the Conway School District. Because the graduating class had over 500 members, for the first time graduation exercises were held at Verizon Arena in nearby North Little Rock. As chairman of the Bookcase Project, I was invited to be present, receive a beautiful plaque, and was given about five minutes on the program to tell the audience of about 12,000 people a little about our project, and our goals and objectives.

What I have just shared with you is at the very heart of why it is important to have a community-wide bookcase project, and not just leave it in the hands of some other group in the community. It is not just about building bookcases and giving them to pre-school children being reared in low-income families. Really, it is more about "awareness" and getting as many literate people as possible to join the fight to defeat illiteracy. Today, in our community there are very few people who have not heard about the Conway Bookcase Project. Working together, over time, we can make a difference. Before I finish this book, I believe you will agree that this is a "winnable" war and you will want to be a part of something that means so much to so many.

Saving Our Nation One Child at a Time

Members of the Conway Bookcase Project Committee shown here with Governer Mike Beebe, when he presented to our committee a "Proclamation" declaring Bookcase Literacy Week in the State of Arkansas.

CHAPTER NINE

THE ANNUAL AWARDS CEREMONY

The most exciting time of our entire bookcase project was about to take place. This is the time when we award the bookcases, along with a starter set of books, to the Head Start children and their parents. The smiles on everyone's face, and the squeals of glee from the children make all the work and effort truly worthwhile. The most satisfying thing for us on the committee and others who are involved in our community is that we know we are making a difference. This has been a team effort all the way, and what started as a simple little ceremony in a church fellowship hall has now become a much-anticipated event that takes place each year in our community.

This is certainly not to minimize the importance of the first Awards Ceremony that took place back in 2005, because we were laying the foundation and developing a pattern that would guide us right up to the present time. Our craftsmen built the bookcases, we collected and

My Heartfelt Passion

sorted the books, and we invited special people to be on the program. The media had also invited the public to come and help us celebrate. That first year, as Chairman of the committee I was honored to be the Emcee. Dr. Larry Pillow give the Invocation, Mayor Tab Townsell gave the Welcome, our Inaugural speaker was Dr. Amanda Moore, Head Librarian at Hendrix College. Mickey Cox presented the bookcases to the children, I gave closing comments to thank everyone, and Dr. Pillow returned to give the Benediction.

We were honored to have tremendous coverage by the media, including the Log Cabin Democrat, Channel 5 Cable Television (that filmed the ceremony for local airing several times), and the Little Rock television stations, KARK Channel 4 (NBC) and KTHV Channel 11 (CBS). I might add, great coverage by the media has continued right up to the present time. The first awards ceremony was now history as the parents loaded the bookcases and books into their cars and trucks after the ceremony and went home. Most, if not all, of these children had never owned their own personal bookcase and, suffice it to say, this was to be the nicest piece of furniture in many of their homes.

We knew that lives were going to be changed forever, and one of the most important things I stressed for parents was for them to buy books and read to their children. This came to fruition a little later when our Head Start director reported that the lending libraries at the centers had a 76 percent increase in parents checking out books to read to their children. And Blanca Ramirez, Literacy Coordinator for Head Start, reports that the trend continues. The foundation was laid and our literacy project was getting more exciting with every passing day, and more people were getting on board to help us.

As it relates to our project, the powerful hand of fate smiled on us once again. The following year, Ruth Voss, Director for the Faulkner County Library System and a member of our committee, invited us to hold our ceremony at the spacious Faulkner County Library here in Conway.

The library has a large center aisle that slopes down to a large open area, which is a perfect place to hold our ceremony. There is even an overhead beam that is a perfect place to hang our large banner that says, "Building a New Generation of Readers." The invitation to hold our ceremony here gave us an anchor, creditability, and the resources to move to the next level.

We now had a great place to hold our event and the library staff was so good to help us with the arrangements, such as setting up 300 chairs, the stage, and public address system. Our craftsmen line up the bookcases, all 50 of them in alphabetical order, along both sides of the aisle, and place a starter set of books in each one. We only give a starter set of 10 to 12 books in order to encourage parents, grandparents and others to give books to the children for special occasions like birthdays and Christmas. This way they are building their very own "personal" library, which is much better than some person or organization giving them a whole bookcase full of books, with many of them being of no interest to the child.

A few years ago, another great blessing came along that we did not plan on. Several people stepped up to provide additional tools that will help the children have a greater passion for reading. The first was Lynnette Cullums, a retired school teacher from Bee Branch, who gave every child a "Children's Bible Story Book" for the first nine years, stopping only when she was forced to the sidelines because of age. Then Crystal Spellman called me one day and wanted to provide a "Reading Buddy" for each of our children. This is a large stuffed toy she personalizes with the child's name, that they can snuggle up to when they are reading. This was especially good for children who have no siblings in the home. And then Patsy Desaulniers volunteered to prepare a bookmark for each child, with a special literacy quote and their name inscribed as well. I am sure you know that little things like this can often make a big difference.

Featured here is the late Lynnette Collums of Bee Branch, Arkansas who gave each of our children a Children's Bible Story book for the first 9 years of our project.

Up to this point I have been describing the "physical" part of our annual literacy event, and now I want to turn our attention to the "people" part, which is far more important. Earlier in the book I stated that my friend Chief Randall Aragon has helped me think outside the box. He felt it was important to have a formal ceremony and invite all the important dignitaries and leaders in our community, somewhat akin to holding a College Graduation Exercise. Who we invited to participate and be on our program was also very important. It was also very important to involve all the members of our committee, who are the real workers and the reason our project is so successful.

Mrs. Crystal Spellman, seen arriving on left, presents each of our children with a "Reading Buddy" each year to go with their personalized bookcase.

As chairman, the first thing I did was compile a list of community leaders, members of our "Bookcase Club" (that I will tell you about in the next chapter), and others who are supportive of our project. We sent them an invitation to our ceremony, giving the date, time, location and who our keynote speaker will be. We wanted them to feel special and also for them to help us spread the message of improving literacy, especially for children being reared in low-income families in our community. Of course, we also hoped they would tell and even send some of their employees to the banquet. These invitations are mailed two to three weeks before the ceremony. We want to get

My Heartfelt Passion

on their busy calendars.

I also began to develop the printed program for the ceremony with help from our committee, to hand to our guests as they arrived. It was here that my years of experience in the printing business really came in handy. While every community is different, we decided that a Sunday afternoon at 3 p.m. was the best time to hold the ceremony because people who attend church would be out, have time to eat, and easily make it to the ceremony. With the ceremony only lasting an hour, there was still time for late afternoon and evening activities.

Here is the order of the program that has evolved over time to highlight our special Awards Ceremony. First, with me serving as the Emcee, the Invocation by a local pastor, then the posting of the colors by our local Junior ROTC Unit from the high school, the Pledge of Allegiance led by a member of our committee, next a word of Welcome by a local officeholder, followed by the introduction for the Keynote Speaker, and the Keynote Address by a noted citizen who is a strong proponent for literacy. Following that is the presentation of the bookcases to the children, and concluding with closing comments from me to express our appreciation for every person's attendance and for helping with the project, and the concluding Benediction by another local pastor.

While you will not recognize most of these names, here is a list of our Keynote Speakers since we began the project back in 2005: Dr. Amanda Moore, college head librarian; Sen. Lu Hardin, university president; Sarah Hunt, Mrs. Arkansas International; Dr. Greg Murry, school superintendent; Ken Hatfield, university head football coach; Dr. Dennis Schick, executive director, Arkansas

Saving Our Nation One Child at a Time

Our Ceremony today is dedicated to the memory of Senator Stanley Russ, faithful member of our Conway Bookcase Project Committee for many years.

Senator Stanley Russ
1930 – 2017

Conway Bookcase Project

Thirteenth Annual Awards Ceremony

A Bookcase for Every Child

Committee Members

Jim Davidson/Chairman *Syndicated Columnist*	Linda Linn *Businesswoman/Civic Leader*
Mickey Cox *Retired/Utility Executive*	Dr. Amanda Moore *Librarian/Career Advisor*
Dr. Tammy Benson *U.C.A. Educator*	Dr. Charlotte Green *Educator/Author*
Cliff Garrison *Retired/Coach & AD*	Don Powell *Business Executive*
Nancy Mitchell *Retired/Teacher*	Kelly Sublett *V.P. of Audience/Newspaper*
Jennifer Welter *Director/CAPCA*	Mark Lollar *Banker/Treasurer*
Caryn Southerland *Children's Author*	John McGraw *Library System Director*

www.bookcaseforeverychild.com

Changing Lives & Futures One at a Time

Sunday, April 23, 2017
3:00 pm
Faulkner County Library
1900 Tyler St., Conway, AR
(3 blocks west of Hendrix College)

This is a copy of our printed program for each of our Annual Awards Ceremonies and is given to each guest as they arrive. This is also a great memento for parents of the children.

Program

Master of Ceremonies	Jim Davidson *Chair, Conway Bookcase Project*
Invocation	Dr. Larry White *Pastor - Woodland Heights Baptist Church*
Presenting of the Colors	Junior ROTC Unit *Conway High School*
Pledge of Allegiance	Jennifer Welter *Member, Conway Bookcase Project*
Welcome	Tim Ryals *Faulkner County Sheriff*
Keynote Speaker	Shawn Hammontree *Christian Ministry*
Presentation of Bookcases	Anna Valenzuela *CAPCA - Head Start Program*
Closing Comments	Jim Davidson
Benediction	Cliff Garrison *Member, Conway Bookcase Project*

America's Greatest Resource ... Her Children

Personalized bookcases and books are presented to the following children with our love and best wishes for a great future.

Annabelle Duckworth	Sukhmeen Kaur
Kaylee Nelson	Zaide Long
Cayden Adams	Mar'Cayla Madden
Hannah Adams	Jaylyn Miranda
Ian Chavez	Rachel Montano
Emily Garcia	Malakhi Parker
Adrian Hernandez	Suliamon Payne
Latrone Humphrey	Naeem Ramos
Terrance Johnson JR.	Faith Silva
Jeremiah King	Jessy Trujillo
Christian Martin	Melody Ward
Ta'vonte McClure	Jayren Zavala
Carsten Osborne	Shirley Childs
Fernando Reboreda	Abrianna Jones
Trestian Smith	Adrian Farmer
Hailey Waddle	Angel Gonzalez
Sharina Wilson	Aniyah Green
Ana Zetino	Jaiden Anderson
Kelis Brown	Jarel Ward
Maria Crisantos	Jaylee Freeman
Genesis Davis	Keegan Alcorn
Olivia Dos Santos	Kennedy Hendricks
Ta'Taris Earnest JR	Landon Moss
Kadeem Graham	London Frazier
Sebastian Hernandez	Jonas Solias

My Heartfelt Passion

Press Association (and magician); Gilbert Baker, former state senator; Dr. Charlotte Green, educator and founder, Arkansas Pre-School Plus literacy program; Kathy Powers, award-winning teacher; Allen Dodson, former county judge; Zach Ahrens, newspaper publisher; Trinina Pouncy, former "Teacher of the Year"; and Shawn Hammontree, church ministry leader. The reason I share these names is to let you know the quality of the people who have helped us encourage our children.

Former Arkansas Razorback Coach Ken Hatfield was the speaker for one of our Annual Award Ceremonies. He was a big hit as he told the children about the "Little Engine That Could."

I have talked throughout the book about the importance of having a community-wide literacy project. Having quality leaders and highly visible people involved in the awards ceremony is the surest way to make this happen. Every single person I have mentioned has a strong center of influence in our community, and by changing the various duties each year with a different person, the circle

Saving Our Nation One Child at a Time

Keynote Speaker Dr. Dennis Schick uses a book to demonstrate the importance of reading for our children, during our Annual Bookcase Awards Ceremony.

Keynote Speaker, Log Cabin Publisher Zach Ahrens, as he speaks to children, parents and guests at our Annual Awards Ceremony.

gets wider and deeper as time goes by. Each year we change the pastor who gives the invocation, the committee member who leads the pledge, the local dignitary who gives the welcome, the person who introduces the keynote speaker, the keynote speaker, and the pastor who gives the closing benediction. This is why today few people in our community have not heard about or been involved in our project in some way.

It should be noted that one of the most important reasons for having a Bookcase Awards Ceremony is what it does for the parents. As a general rule, most low-income people do not have much to celebrate, as they receive very little positive recognition in the community, including in the form of honors and awards. Our primary goal is to make each one of them feel special, because they are special, they were created in the image of God. When individuals truly feel better about themselves, their attitude, behavior, self-confidence and self-worth will begin to reflect it, and what is even more exciting is that they see the potential and want what's better for their children. And it is equally important that they see and feel the love and concern of other people.

To be sure, our project is providing a great literacy tool in the form of a quality bookcase for these children; but believe it or not, the greatest impact comes from the fact the child's name is on it. It has been said that a person's name is the sweetest and most important sound in any language. This says to the child, "This is mine, it belongs to me," the same feeling millions of Americans have when they own their own house, or car or many other things. The pride of ownership is a great motivator for people who have very little, and being able to read and communicate

Saving Our Nation One Child at a Time

is a really terrific way for these special children to share in the American dream.

Conway Bookcase Project

> *The Conway Bookcase Project Committee*
>
> *Enthusiastically invites you to attend the*
>
> ### *Thirteenth Annual Awards Ceremony*
>
> Sunday, April 23, 2017
> 3:00 PM
>
> *Faulkner County Library*
> *1900 Tyler Street*
> *Conway, Arkansas*
> *(West of Hendrix College)*
>
> *Keynote Speaker will be*
> **Shawn Hammontree**
> **Christian Ministry**
>
> *Books and Bookcases will be*
> *Presented to children and their parents*
>
> *Jim Davidson, Chairman*
> *1-501-499-2179 or email: jimdavidson@conwaycorp.net*
> **www.bookcaseforeverychild.com**

A personal invitation is sent to over 200 supporters and others asking them to attend our Annual Awards Ceremony. This is the copy we use and may provide a template.

My Heartfelt Passion

Men who are strong supporters of our project, Stanley Russ, Mickey Cox, Jim Davidson, Joe Ward, Jerry Glover and Jason Wynkoop waiting for the ceremony to begin.

Here former State Senator Stanley Russ, Phyliss Fry and Leo Treat have come to help us celebrate literacy, and to support Head Start parents and children.

Saving Our Nation One Child at a Time

A portion of the crowd at our Tenth Annual Bookcase Awards Ceremony at the Faulkner County Library.

Founder Jim Davidson welcomes the crowd at our Annual Bookcase Awards Ceremony at the Faulkner County Library.

My Heartfelt Passion

Master Craftsman Mickey Cox, seen here as he presents fifty bookcases and a starter set of books, to parents and their children.

Committee Member Dr. Larry Pillow leads us in the "Pledge" as High School ROTC members present the colors at our ceremony.

Saving Our Nation One Child at a Time

A "Head Start" child as she stands beside her very own personalized, bookcase at our Annual Awards Ceremony.

Bookcase "Reading Buddies" bookcases and books waiting for parents and children to take them home, to begin a new life of reading.

My Heartfelt Passion

This is copy for our "Founders" note card that is sent to say "Thank You" to volunteers and supporters. It is very important to personally thank these wonderful people.

Conway Bookcase Project
2 Bentley Drive
Conway, AR 72034

CHAPTER TEN
THE BOOKCASE FUNDRAISING BANQUET

There was a day and time in our country, several decades ago, when the vast majority of families ate almost all of their meals together. Each family member would be seated "in their place" around the table. This was a time not only for delicious home-cooked meals, but to discuss the events of the day and a time when parents taught their children manners, etiquette and the importance of having and maintaining good character values.

In this regard, I have noted that something almost magical happens when people place their feet under the same dinner table and share quality food that nourishes and satisfies them. We are seldom happier than when we are eating and having good fellowship with family and friends (and that includes young people who seem to be attached to their electronic devices). It is in this spirit that I believe the Lord gave me the best fund-raising idea that

My Heartfelt Passion

I have ever received for our bookcase project, an annual Bookcase Fundraising Banquet.

To an annual Bookcase Fundraising Banquet we would invite our supporters and others who truly understand the importance of literacy to join us for a delicious meal and some quality "local" entertainment. Here, of course, our purpose, conversation and the focus of the evening would be literacy and how we can help children being reared in low-income homes to have a better future. When I shared this idea with our committee, they were equally enthusiastic about doing it. Each member got on board and soon preparation was under way.

This is the cafeteria at Bob & Betty Courtway Middle School where we hold our Annual Bookcase Literacy Banquet. With seating of over 400, it is a perfect place to hold this event..

The first order of business was to find a great place to hold this event. Almost by fate, my next-door neighbor was the assistant principal at the Bob & Betty Courtway Middle School, one of two public middle schools in our community. This school has a large cafeteria with a great kitchen and staff to run it. With seating of over 400, it was perfect and they welcomed us with open arms. This was in 2008 and we have been there ever since. Thinking back, this was a natural choice as it is a neutral site where everyone feels comfortable and the vast majority of children who would receive bookcases will later attend school there. Most communities have these same kinds of meeting accommodations and will welcome your great literacy project as well.

The next item on our agenda was to set the date and time for the banquet. There were a number of factors that entered into this decision. First, we wanted to build and present the bookcases to the children in the same school year, which generally runs from mid-August to the following end of May. We decided to hold our banquet the third week of October at 6:30 p.m. on a Thursday, in order to avoid the Friday evening football games when local teams were playing. The banquet must take place before we have the Awards Ceremony in the spring to present the bookcases because this ensures we have the money to purchase the building materials.

We also knew from the beginning that it would be necessary to develop a timeline of tasks. Some tasks needed to be taken care of well ahead of the event, others as we moved closer, and still others had to be done the day of the banquet before guests arrived. It is important to involve every member of our committee, not only to use their skills and talents to ensure our success, but also to spread the workload around. What follows, in sequence, are the details and tasks that were handled in a very efficient manner. We use a written checklist to make sure we don't forget anything, and encourage you to do the same.

First, to provide pertinent information to the newspaper and other media outlets so they could begin to promote our Inaugural Banquet. Next, we determined the price of each ticket to be $15.95, the cost of my book that we sold to raise money the first three years, before starting our banquet. Then, thanks to a suggestion from one of our committee members, we offered a "table of tickets" for $125. This proved to be very helpful, and individuals, banks and other businesses all over town bought a table of tickets, even if they could not attend. We now sell about 40 of these tables each year and this makes it possible to have over 400 guests in attendance. This provides more than enough money to build the bookcases.

We provided the information to our local copy shop and they developed our tickets. We print them six on a side, and 80 sheets of 8 ½ by 11 cover stock yields 480 tickets, more than enough for our needs. A copy of the ticket is shown with the photos so you can see it. We also have "tent-cards" on each table showing the sponsor's name on both sides, and we use the heading "Compliments Of" rather than "Sponsored by" because this makes our guests feel comfortable to sit anywhere they choose. This is a great concept for our sponsors because many of them consider this as good advertising. One word of caution: in election years you will have a good number of candidates for office who purchase tables of tickets. Just remember that literacy is not a partisan issue, so be careful not to

Saving Our Nation One Child at a Time

BANQUET TICKET

Come Dine with Us
At our Ninth Annual
Bookcase Literacy Banquet
Hosted by the

Conway Bookcase Project Committee

**Tuesday, October 18, 2016 - 6:30 P.M.
Bob & Betty Courtway Middle School Cafeteria
1200 Bob Courtway Drive – Conway**

Enjoy a meal for the price of a book.
Cost $15.95 per person with proceeds to build bookcases for children in low-income families.

No need to reinvent the wheel as this copy of our "banquet ticket" can be adapted for your use. We print those 6 up, front and back and 80 sheets of cover stock yields 480 tickets.

For your donation, you will receive:

- A delicious meal – Catfish & All the Trimmings
- Great entertainment –
  Craig O'Neill, Channel 11 Television
- A complimentary copy of Founder
  Jim Davidson's book "New Revised Edition of Learning, Earning & Giving Back"
- The satisfaction of knowing you are helping to provide a quality personalized bookcase for children in low-income families.
- Be provided with an opportunity to donate "gently used" children's books.

**Please make checks payable to
Conway Bookcase Project.
www.bookcaseforeverychild.com**

My Heartfelt Passion

Conway Bookcase Project

Ninth Annual Bookcase Literacy Fundraiser Banquet Hosted by the

Conway Bookcase Project Committee
Tuesday, October 18th, 2016: 6:30 P.M.
Bob & Betty Courtway Middle School Cafeteria
Proceeds to build bookcases
Tickets 15.95 each or table of 8 for $125.00

Catfish & All the Trimmings

Entertainment by: Craig O'Neill – Channel 11 Television

Tickets also available at the Log Cabin Democrat, Faulkner County Library, Conway Copies, or call Jim Davidson: 499-2179, Stanley Russ: 329-8186, Dr. Tammy Benson: 501-852-2965 or Judy Lovell: 501-327-7482 for tickets.

Order Form

I would like _____ tickets ($15.95 ea.) or a "Table of 8 Tickets" ($125.00) to attend the Ninth Annual Bookcase Fundraiser Literacy Banquet

Name: _____

jimdavidson@conwaycorp.net   www.bookcaseforeverychild.com

This is a preregister form to include with your "Bookcase Club" letter many other needs to sell tickets and solicit 'Table Sponsors" from across the community.

Saving Our Nation One Child at a Time

The Conway Bookcase Project Committee
Welcomes You To The
Ninth Annual Bookcase Literacy Banquet

Agenda

Old Favorite Piano Selections by Janis Davidson
Welcome: Jim Davidson, Chairman
Invocation: Dr. Michael Roberts
Dinner- Enjoy & Fellowship
Entertainment: Craig O'Neill – Channel 11 Television
Closing Comments & Benediction: Jim Davidson

Table Sponsors

Conway Corporation * Judge Jim Baker * First Security Bank * Log Cabin Democrat * University Church of Christ * Friends of the Library * Simmons Bank* Central Baptist College * Conway Regional Health System * UCA - Kappa Delta Pi * Senator Jason Rapert * CAPCA * Senator Stanley Russ * First Service Bank * Farm Bureau Insurance * Centennial Bank * Rep. Steve Magie * Bank of the Ozarks * Dave & Jean Leffler * Regions Bank * Conway Copies * JSI Metal & Electronic Recycling * Arvest Bank * Conway Rotary Club * Laureate Alpha Omega Chapter of Beta Sigma Phi * Conway Noon Lions Club * Conway Kiwanis Club * Pickles Gap Village * David Meeks State Rep * David & Janis Elms * Coach Cliff Garrison * Doretta Bright * Conway High School Key Club * Young at Heart Class * Central Baptist Church * Tim Ryals for Sheriff * Bart Castleberry for Mayor * Bear State Bank

Our Mission

Since beginning in 2005, the members of the Conway Bookcase Project Committee, with bountiful help from our community, have built and presented 600 quality, personalized oak bookcases, and a starter set of books, to pre-school children in the Conway Head-Start Program. We are an all volunteer project and use no tax money or grants of any kind. We are truly about "Giving Back" and we are all dedicated to improving literacy among children in disadvantaged homes. Your presence here tonight will enable us to build 50 more bookcases to be presented in April 2017, and to provide "seed" money for other local projects, here in Arkansas, and across the nation, that will enable them to start their own "Bookcase for Every Child" project.

Thank You, Conway Bookcase Project Committee

Committee Members: Jim Davidson - Chair, Cliff Garrison, Mickey Cox, Senator Stanley Russ, Dr. Amanda Moore, Linda Linn, Nancy Mitchell, Dr. Tammy Benson, Caryn Southerland, Jennifer Welter, John McGraw, Don Powell, Dr. Charlotte Green, Kelly Sublett & Mark Lollar.

This is copy for our Annual Bookcase Literacy Banquet agenda. It is printed on several bright colors of bond paper, and placed at each table setting.

My Heartfelt Passion

Conway Bookcase Project
2 Bentley Drive * Conway, AR 72034

The Bookcase Club
(By invitation only)

September 12, 2016

Dear Pat,

Our 9th Annual "Bookcase Fundraising Banquet" is scheduled for Tuesday, October 18th, 6:30 p.m., at the Bob & Betty Courtway Middle School Cafeteria. At this time we will raise the funds to build 50 more quality, personalized bookcases for pre-school children being reared in **low-income families** in our community.

These are the children who truly need our help because statistics tell us that most of these children have no books in their home to read, before they start to school. This will make a total of 650 bookcases, and books, we have given since our project began in 2005, and **we are making a difference.**

As in the past, as a member of The Bookcase Club I would like to invite you to contribute a non-tax deductible donation of $50 to help buy the food for our banquet. This means that all the proceeds from the banquet can be used to buy the wood and supplies to build the bookcases.

This year our speaker will be Craig O'Neill, from Channel 11 Television, who is a strong supporter of literacy. Unless preempted by late breaking news, Craig will do a 'live shot' during the evening newscast. By popular request we are changing our menu to catfish, and all the trimmings, and my wife Janis will play "old favorites" on the piano, to welcome our guests as they arrive. It will be a fun evening for a great cause.

God bless you for helping these kids. Please make checks payable to **Conway Bookcase Project** and return in the self-addressed stamped envelope and the ticket form if you plan to attend. This being a national election year, many public officials will be in attendance.

We are grateful for your help,

Jim Davidson, Founder
/enc.

www.bookcaseforeverychild.com

This letter is mailed to about 50 "Bookcase Club" members, about 30 days before the banquet takes place. Add a self-addressed stamped envelope and registration form for great response.

favor one candidate or party over another. Arrange your banquet seating accordingly.

After a few years of holding the banquet, I had another good idea that proved to be very helpful, to develop a "Bookcase Club" to help pay for the cost of the food. This allows all the proceeds from our banquet ticket sales to be used to buy wood and supplies. The idea is to identify people of means in the community who, because of schedule or health, cannot be directly involved but want to be a part of our great literacy project. They are asked to contribute $50 each year to help in this way. Some contribute even more. It did not take long to come up with a list of about 50 people who fit this category. We placed their names on mailing labels and then developed a personal letter, exclusively for "Bookcase Club" members.

About a month before the banquet, a letter is mailed to the members. We send this letter along with a flyer giving details of the banquet, and a self-addressed stamped envelope so they can return their check to us. The self-addressed stamped envelope makes it easy for the members to write their check and get it back in the mail. This has worked wonderfully well and we raise about $1,500 each year that defrays the cost of food, and is another great way for more people to be involved.

One of the tenets of our project is to involve as many people as possible to help fight illiteracy. At this time, we have had between 4,000 and 5,000 of our citizens directly involved in one way or another. This allows each individual person to be of service. While they are not put into practice until the day of the banquet, there are a number of details

My Heartfelt Passion

that must be taken care of several days in advance. For the first eight years we enlisted volunteers to work in the kitchen and prepare a delicious meal of smoked sausage, spaghetti, kraut, slaw, French bread, coffee, tea and water. However, we began to get complaints that the food was too spicy. It was time for a change, plus the fact that finding good cooks to work in the kitchen year after year was the hardest part of the project to sustain.

So we switched our menu and had our meal catered by a local restaurant — catfish and all the trimmings. They only charged $7 per plate so we had plenty of money left to purchase materials. We still have several good cooks each prepare approximately 25 desserts at home and bring them to the banquet. We rotate students between the three school districts in our community and invite about 10 students to serve drinks and dessert to our guests. Our local churches are also a good source for workers and you will have more help than you need. Just ask.

Another important item is the evening's entertainment. You will find many local or nearby groups who are happy to lend a hand and perform for a benefit to help improve literacy. We only use "family-friendly" entertainment by selecting groups that play gospel, country, bluegrass or big band music, since (1) we want our guests to leave feeling inspired and committed to help spread the word about helping children in low-income families learn to read, and (2) many families, including children, come to the banquet.

Some of the many musical groups we have had entertain our guests include, Senator Jason Rapert and

Saving Our Nation One Child at a Time

State Senator Jason Rapert is well known in our area for his Fiddle playing. He and his band, shown here, performed for our Inaugural Bookcase Literacy Banquet in October of 2008.

Our bookcase project is all about community involvement. Featured here are members of the Conway High School Jazz Band as they perform for guests at a Bookcase Literacy Banquet.

his Bluegrass Band, the Ward Family Gospel Singers, Conway Symphony Orchestra, Conway High School Jazz Band, Conway Women's Chorus, Dr. Bill Higgs ("Ukulele Man"), and The Davanzo Family. At our most recent banquet we changed gears, and had television personality and comedian Craig O'Neill from CBS Channel 11. He did a fantastic job, keeping everyone laughing while still relating to our mission. Many said he was our best program ever. As our guests arrived, my wife Janis, an accomplished pianist, played popular tunes on the piano for about 30 minutes to set the mood for a great evening.

Now, it is the day of the event, and about all that is left to do is to check the sound system and decorate the banquet room with a literacy theme. This includes having a couple of sample bookcases set up for our guests to see. To add a little cheer, on the tables we use bright-colored table cloths, colored paper with our evening's agenda at each place setting, books, ABC blocks, and floral arrangements with fall colors. We also have some decorated boxes for guests to deposit books we asked them to bring and donate. As our guests arrive they are greeted by two of our committee members, who sit at a small table near the front door to sell or take tickets. We have other committee members who greet and help them find a place to sit. The atmosphere we strive to create is for everyone to have fun and feel comfortable and good about being there for a great cause.

We are also pleased to report that each year since our project began we have raised more money than we have needed to build bookcases, and our bank account has continued to grow. Today we are in excellent financial shape. From the beginning I have had a policy of my only putting money "in" the account but never taking any money "out", that is handled by our treasurer, who is a banker. He works for one of the largest banks in our community and does an excellent job of writing checks and paying all the bills that keep us current.

Members of our original Conway Bookcase Project Committee pose for a photo at the end of our First Bookcase Literacy Banquet. They are the best.

Our committee gets most of the credit for the success of our project, and we have had a number of new people come on board since we began in 2005. Only five original members remain, and this is good because new members bring vitality and new ideas to share with us. Here are our current committee members, and the expertise which each provides for the project. I list them to show the breadth and depth of expertise, talent, and support we need and are

My Heartfelt Passion

proud to have. I encourage you to seek out and recruit similar kinds of people. Jim Davidson (Chairman), syndicated columnist; Mickey Cox, retired utility executive; Dr. Tammy Benson, University of Central Arkansas educator; Cliff Garrison, retired coach and athletic director; Nancy Mitchell, retired teacher; Jennifer Welter, Director, Community Action Program for Central Arkansas (Head Start); Caryn Southerland, children's author; Linda Linn, businesswoman and civic leader; Dr. Amanda Moore, librarian and career adviser; Dr. Charlotte Green, educator and author; Don Powell, business executive; Kelly Sublett, newspaper vice president of audience; John McGraw, library system director; and Mark Lollar, (treasurer), banker.

A Simple Truth: It is a lot easier to get where we want to go if someone else has already built the road or laid the track. And with this thought, a special word of thanks to Dr. Dennis Schick and Colleen Holt for editing this book, and to Kirk Jordan, Leo Treat and Paul Foster for taking the photos.

Saving Our Nation One Child at a Time

At each of our Annual Bookcase Literacy Banquets, we proudly display some finished bookcases so our supporters can see the quality of workmanship our craftsmen are doing.

We invite supporters of our Conway Bookcase Project to bring new or "gently used" children's books to our bookcase banquets. They will be presented to our children the following spring.

My Heartfelt Passion

Former State Senator Gilbert Baker is shown here trying to find a seat at one at one of our recent Bookcase Literacy Banquets. We all come together each year for the cause of literacy.

The late former Senator Stanley Russ was a community treasure. We were blessed to have him Emcee our bookcase banquets for many years. Here he speaks to a large appreciative crowd.

Saving Our Nation One Child at a Time

Featured in this photo is Luis Ortega who developed and hosts our website: www.bookcaseforeverychild.com and Ken Ingram an architect who drew the bookcase plans.

Janis Davidson has been playing the piano for over six decades and does a wonderful job of warming up the audience getting ready for our Annual Bookcase Literacy Banquet.

My Heartfelt Passion

Dr. Charlotte Green adds a touch of class as Emcee of our Annual Bookcase Literacy Banquet. She is the Founder of Arkansas Preschool Plus, an associate of the Dolly Parton Imagination Library.

Little Rock television personality, Craig O'Neill, as he entertains the crowd at our Annual Bookcase Literacy Banquet. He did a fantastic job of promoting literacy for all those in attendance.

Saving Our Nation One Child at a Time

Janis Davidson and long-time friend Dr. Ben McNew seen here getting ready for catfish and all the trimmings at our annual banquet.

One of our strongest committee members, Dr. Larry Pillow, seen here with his lovely wife Peggy, as they enjoy the hospitality at a recent bookcase banquet.

My Heartfelt Passion

Coach Cliff Garrison and Dr. Charlotte Green are faithful members of our committee and Charlotte has served as banquet Emcee for the past several years.

Founder Jim Davidson and Craig O'Neill seen here before our Ninth Annual Bookcase Literacy Banquet. Craig had Jim on KTHV Channel 11 Television a few days earlier to promote attendance at the event.

Saving Our Nation One Child at a Time

We are greatful for each perosn who attends our events, and especially for great cooks who prepare our homemade desserts.

My Heartfelt Passion

Our great joy is giving bookcases and books to some very special children and we are blessed to have craftsmen from other cities who build them.

THE AMERICAN PROFILE STOPS BY

CHAPTER ELEVEN

THE AMERICAN PROFILE STOPS BY

Former Secretary of Agriculture E.T. Meredith once said, "The man who fails to advertise just because conditions are a little uncertain is on par with the farmer who refuses to feed his cows because the price of butter has gone down." This is another way of saying there is not much chance for success unless we let other people know what we are selling or doing, and what the benefits are for them.

When it comes to advertising or promoting our Bookcase for Every Child project, we found a good friend back in 2011 when the American Profile magazine stopped by and featured our project with a front page cover story. While we did not realize it at the time, as the old saying goes, "This was just what the doctor ordered."

The Bible says, "Where there is no vision the people perish." If you have read my book to this point I believe you will agree that I do have a vision, and that is to make a difference in the lives of millions of pre-school children being reared in low-income families. These are the children with the greatest risk of failure because they do not have the necessary tools to achieve real success.

We had been having a successful bookcase project for six years when Alan English, the former publisher of our local daily newspaper, Log Cabin Democrat, told a friend who worked for American Profile magazine about our project and they decided to do a feature story about us. This newspaper magazine was published in Franklin, Tennessee. and it had a staff of contributing editors and photographers who traveled all across the county, featuring some really great stories about what people and organizations are doing in their local communities.

It was a big day for us when American Profile Contributing Editor Marti Attoun and photographer David Mudd came to Conway to do a story about our project. The front-page story ran in the July 31 – August 6, 2011, issue and featured on the cover student Nija Graves, one of the children who received a personalized bookcase back in 2005. This newspaper magazine, often called a Sunday supplement, was inserted in hundreds of newspapers throughout the country. In 2014 it was sold to Athlon, which also purchased Parade magazine. American Profile still exists, with the added words, Community Table. But when they ran our story they had a readership of over 10 million. In our case they were really first class, and also produced a video featuring Nija, her mother Sherry, Mickey Cox and myself telling our story that brought our project up close and personal. The story and video were featured on their website, where people all across America could see what we were doing here in Conway.

Saving Our Nation One Child at a Time

My Heartfelt Passion

[COVER STORY]

A Bookcase for Every Child

BY MARTI ATTOUN, CONTRIBUTING EDITOR   PHOTOS BY DAVID MUDD

Watch the bookcase project in action at americanprofile.com/bookcaseforeverychild

Arkansas town promotes literacy one kid at a time

HUGGING HER STUFFED LAMB, Nija Graves, 5, picks one of her favorite books, *Rain, Rain*, from a handcrafted oak bookcase personalized with her name, then tells her mother that she's ready to read.

"We read every evening," says Sherry Graves, 46, of Conway, Ark. (pop. 43,167). "Sometimes Nija says, 'Will you read me five books?' She always wants more books."

Nija is among 350 Conway children who have received free bookcases stocked with books since 2005, thanks to A Bookcase for Every Child, a project started by Jim Davidson and run like clockwork by a team of community volunteers.

"We do the bookcase project because we care. We love these kids," says Davidson, 72, of Conway, a syndicated newspaper columnist whose concern about illiteracy inspired him to create the bookcase project.

Spreading the joy

"Parental and community involvement is the only way to improve literacy," says Davidson, who came up with the idea to spread the joy of reading by building and providing custom-made bookcases and starter libraries of a dozen books to 3- and 4-year-olds enrolled in Head Start, a federal program that promotes education among preschoolers from low-income households where books may be scarce and parents sometimes struggle with reading.

"The primary purpose of this bookcase project is to encourage and help parents in disadvantaged families to read to and with their children," says Davidson, who donates the proceeds from his book of columns, *Learning, Earning & Giving Back*, to the literacy project. "If these young kids don't get the language foundation, vocabulary and communication skills they need, they're behind before they ever start to school."

Since Davidson launched the project, more than 2,000 volunteers in Conway have kept it aloft. They bake cakes and grill sausages for the Bookcase Literacy Banquet each October to raise money for wood and other supplies to build the bookcases. They collect and sort thousands of donated books, cut and sand boards, assemble and stain the bookcases, and affix personalized brass nameplates.

Volunteer Mickey Cox, 71, of Conway, devotes about three weeks each March helping build 50 bookcases. "It's a grand
(Continued on page 8)

// Nija Graves keeps her books in a personalized bookcase built by volunteers in Conway, Ark.

Continued from page 6
community thing to do," says Cox, a retired utility company executive. "I look at the inability to read as like being in a prison without bars. You're totally dependent on other people to tell you something when you can't read."

The highlight for Cox is watching appreciative youngsters accept their bookcases at a banquet in their honor each April at the Faulkner County Public Library in Conway. "We see their eyes light up," he says. "It makes you feel good to help."

Borrowed books

As intended, the bookcase project is spurring family reading at home, says Tiffany Baker, a coordinator at the Community Action Program for Central Arkansas, which oversees Head Start. Since the project began, the number of books borrowed from the agency's lending library has more than doubled.

"Children bring their parents in to pick out a book and say, 'Hey, that's what I want to read tonight,'" says Baker, 32. "We're seeing more parent involvement in reading."

Such enthusiastic support for A Bookcase for Every Child from recipients and volunteers is a point of pride for Davidson. "The project doesn't cost taxpayers a penny and can leapfrog across the country," he says.

Three dollars from each $15.95 banquet ticket is set aside as seed money to spread the program to other communities. Davidson has helped start programs in El Dorado, Ark. (pop. 21,530), Stuttgart, Ark. (pop. 9,745) and Wynne, Ark. (pop. 8,615), and has compiled instructions covering every phase of the project to assist other communities.

"Each year we're reaching out to more people," Davidson says. "Someday, we could have A Bookcase for Every Child in every state."

And that could translate into a storybook beginning for children like Nija, who can't wait to open another book. ★

// Jim Davidson (left) and Mickey Cox spearhead A Bookcase for Every Child, a community project designed to spread the joy of reading.

Saving Our Nation One Child at a Time

Marti and David went to the Graves home, where Sherry and Nija had her bookcase and books on display. They told about reading each evening, how much her bookcase had helped her schoolwork and how it had helped to develop a passion for books and for reading. The end result of the project that first year goes far beyond this one child as intended. The bookcase project is spurring family reading at home, says Tiffany Baker, a coordinator at CAPCA Head Start. Since the project began, the number of books borrowed from the agency's lending library has more than doubled. "Children bring their parents to pick out a book and say, 'Hey, that's what I want to read tonight'," says Baker. "We're seeing more parent involvement in reading," a key element in the success of the project.

Over the years there is one thing I have noticed about each person who is truly involved in our project, and that is the deep satisfaction they receive from helping those who are less fortunate. There is no greater feeling in the world than what comes from helping those who cannot help themselves, and who could never repay us for what we have done for them. This came to mind when I read a note from Pat Ross, Chairman of the Bridgeport, Texas, Bookcase Project. He said, "We usually have the mother of a child who received a bookcase and books from the previous year speak at the presentation. It is hard not to shed a tear while listening to their stories. I cannot tell you how grateful I am to have discovered you and the program. It has brought me a great pleasure as one of my retirement projects."

While doing research for this book, I discovered that we now have a total of nine projects in six states that are building bookcases and giving books to children from

My Heartfelt Passion

low-income families. The American Profile magazine article is responsible for projects in several other states. In Cleveland, Oklahoma, Mayor Ron Shipman is the Chairman. They have built and presented over 100 bookcases to date. The project in Bridgeport, Texas, I just told you about has built and presented 300 bookcases. We have a project in Oneonta, New York, headed by Marie Lusins and they have built 101 bookcases so far.

Still another project that was inspired by the American Profile article is in DeKalb, Illinois, and is headed by John Rey. Several years after starting the project, he ran for Mayor, and with four candidates in the race, won without a runoff. John has done a fantastic job, and the DeKalb/Sycamore project can serve as a model of the way a project should be organized and run year by year. John says, "Jim, we completed our sixth annual Literacy Banquet on February 9th. Good support is still present in DeKalb/Sycamore for the cause of literacy. We build 50 bookcases each year and this will make 300 since we began our project. Approximately 35 Bookcase Club member donors underwrote our banquet. Attendance was about 150 to 200 people. Our entertainment was provided by high school music students who did a great job.

Two Rivers Head Start is glad to have us as a community partner! Local DeKalb County Housing Authority donates space for collection/storage of books. Barnes & Noble donates books collected over the holiday season for our cause. We have numerous community donors of books as well. A local United Methodist church donates space to us during the month of April for sorting books. Jerry Johns Literacy Clinic of Northern Illinois University (NIU) provides members of its Educator's Club to assist with sorting. They make quick work of the task.

We engage Northern University students (primarily Education majors) in assistance with sorting books and reading to children at the Awards Ceremony after presenting their bookcases. Our Awards ceremony is scheduled for May 6th and is hosted at our local banquet center. Families are invited (extended families usually attend) and this brings a diverse portion of our community together in a venue they otherwise would never see. The project is a great community builder. NIU education majors read to small groups of children that afternoon, during refreshments following the ceremony. It is rewarding to see the bright, faces on the children when they come forward to receive their very own personalized bookcase."

There is one more out-of-state project I want to tell you about. Police Chief Randall Aragon helped start a Bookcase Project in Fairbanks, Alaska, and even though he is no longer there it will be continued by Mike Kolasa, who tells me the bookcases will be made by a man who makes dog mushing sleds – a real woodworker. They have built 20 bookcases thus far and Mike is committed to helping us spread the project in his state.

We have four projects here in Arkansas so far, including Conway, where we have built 650 bookcases. We have a project in Wynne, headed by Sherry Breckenridge, and they have built 513 bookcases. We have a project in Greenbrier headed by Marilyn Battles and Shawn Hammontree, where they have built 177 bookcases. And we have a project in Mayflower, headed by Mike Raney, where they have built 153 bookcases. With a little simple math you can see the total number is well over 2,000 bookcases, with a starter set of books given to some very special children.

You may ask, "What size city/town/community do you need to live in to begin a Bookcase for Every Child project?" Obviously, just as each individual person is unique, every city/town/community is also unique. A good rule of thumb is to have towns that are county seat towns or towns of similar size, or larger. Larger cities with more people have tremendous resources, of course. But while major cities need bookcase projects more than practically anyone, it seems to me that it would be more difficult to begin a project where people don't even know their next-door neighbor. However, many large cities also have close-knit suburbs, and they may work well. Here, a little common sense will go a long way.

Yes, the American Profile cover story was a major boost for our project. But it was the people who read about it and were inspired by it who got projects started in their communities. Of course, we would welcome similar publicity from other media, whether local, regional or national. Please contact me if you have any ideas or leads to pursue.

And here is an offer from the Bookcase for Every Child project as a little incentive. Just get the right people on board, the project under way with a name, chairperson, treasurer, and bank account, and we will send you a set of the bookcase building plans free of charge. Other than this book, the best source of information is our website: www.bookcaseforeverychild.com. To get the ball rolling, please e-mail me at jimdavidson@conwaycorp.net

CHAPTER TWELVE

A CALL TO ACTION

We have been providing quality, personalized bookcases and a starter set of books to Head Start children since we began our project back in 2005. Almost from the beginning we all wanted to know the answer to the question, "Does this really make any difference in the lives of these children?" Well, I can tell you the answer to this question is a resounding "YES"!! It does make a difference, as shown in the following message from Jennifer Welter, our local CAPCA Head Start director, posted on Facebook the day of our 13th annual Awards Ceremony. I believe you will agree.

"Thanks to Mr. Jim Davidson, the Bookcase for Every Child project has been promoting literacy for 13 years! I have always known what a blessing the Project was, but hearing from a former Head Start child (who received a bookcase in 2005 and is now a sophomore in High School) tell his personal story was touching. This driven young man

My Heartfelt Passion

already has scholarship offers! He gives credit to reading and in part to the Bookcase Project! Seeing the impact of handcrafted personalized bookcases with a starter set of books in the homes of low-income children is making a difference."

The greatest reward we all receive is knowing we are making a difference in the lives of some very special children. Here Jovoni Johnson tells us we have made a difference in his life.

We have had a wonderful relationship with this Head Start program since our project was founded, and this includes with former directors Phyliss Fry and Archie Musselman. The day of our ceremony we also heard student Jovoni Johnson say, "I was 4 years of age and passing my bookcase every day and saw my name on it. I finally decided I wanted to read and have some more books in my bookcase. However, my mother told me that I could only have books in my bookcase that I had read." Well, he continued to read and found that he loved reading, and soon his bookcase was overflowing. He found a love for reading, and future success that he would never have realized without his own bookcase and our being there for him. This made a big impact on me and all the others who were in attendance. As I told the crowd that day, "This is what our project is all about."

From this point forward I would like to suspend the narrative for a bit and just talk with you from my heart. You have read my story and how I came to have a real passion for children being reared in low-income homes, and in most cases entering school without a good foundation for achieving success and staying in school. In the past few days, this has really been brought home to me and thousands of others who live here in Central Arkansas. The television stations, radio stations and newspapers have been reporting a wave of violence, including several murders from drive-by shootings that have taken place on the streets of our capital city of Little Rock. It has gotten so bad the mayor and law enforcement authorities have been holding public meetings, asking local citizens to attend and offer suggestions as to the best way to deal with this tragic problem.

One young lady stated her opinion that the problem stems from the youth having nothing to do and recommending that the authorities structure programs in gyms and on baseball fields to keep them busy. It was also pointed out that there were so few jobs these young people could find to earn some money. I say young people because most of them are just kids, under 25 years of age and either graduating or dropping out of school. One thing I seldom hear in meetings of this type is the terrible problem of illiteracy. It would be rather difficult to prove this, but I suspect that the vast majority of those who are involved in drive-by shootings and other forms of violence have very poor literacy skills.

One thing for sure, I have never heard anyone comment that these people should be reading books to better themselves, rather than riding around shooting up the town and murdering innocent people. The simple truth of the matter is this: readers are winners and most illiterates are losers. You, me and every other literate American citizen has the power to change this, at least for future generations. As one concerned citizen to another, I am asking you to get involved by talking with other people in your town or city about starting a Bookcase for Every Child project. It is all about "giving back." We all can help have a better nation and future for our children and grandchildren.

You know you are on the right track when the Arkansas Campaign for Grade Level Reading (AR-GLR) reports that tests show only 31 percent of third graders are reading at grade level. You can do the math, but this means that 69 percent of our state's third graders are not reading at the desired benchmark for their grade level. While some states may be doing better than this, I bet most have similar educational problems as we have here in Arkansas. One thing I can promise you is that if every child had been given a personalized bookcase and a starter set of books when they were 4 years old, this would not be the case. This is such a small investment when you think about the future of a child and also the future of our nation.

The real question for me has become, "How will we get the word out to millions of Americans who can help to change this dire picture?" To be sure, we need a plan, which is why I am issuing this "Call to Action." You may be sure that many of us are committed. I will be happy to give national television interviews, make speeches, and encourage people to visit our website. My wife, who is a Facebook whiz, will promote our cause there. And with your help we all can encourage as many of our literate citizens as possible to read this book, and then to act. I believe you will agree that it tells the story and how we can, working together, make a difference in the months and years to come. You can help if you know media people who can give us some great publicity.

A Personal Challenge from Jim Davidson

A part of good American citizenship is "giving back" and making a contribution to the future of our nation. There is no better way to do this than making it possible for children in low-income families to develop good literacy skills to be able to read, write and communicate. In some measure this will insure they have the opportunity to succeed in life and carry on the traditions that have made our nation the greatest in the history of mankind. What makes the Bookcase for Every Child project so appealing and valuable is that we require the use of no tax money or grants of any kind.

The people in positions of leadership, and especially our nation's policy makers, are those who get things done. Therefore, my challenge is to the President of the United States, members of Congress, our Nation's Governors, members of our State Legislatures and the leaders and policy makers in counties, cities and towns all across this great land.

Before I bring this book to a close, there is another matter of the heart that I would like to share with you. In 2013, I lost my wife Viola, after a 19-year battle with Parkinson's disease. Naturally, this was a very sad time for me, but by the grace of God and the help of my family and friends, I was able to reach a state of perfect peace. This is because I knew in my heart that I had given her excellent care in the final months, weeks and days of her life. And I knew for sure where she was going and that I would see her again.

However, after a couple of years I began to be lonely and I also needed someone to help me continue the various ministries I was involved in, namely the Bookcase for Every Child project, Reach Youth for Christ, and my weekly newspaper column. One day I asked the Lord to send me a Godly Spirit-filled woman who would love me and be enthusiastic about continuing the work I was doing. True to His word, Philippians 4:19 says, "But my God shall supply all you need according to His riches in glory in Christ Jesus." And does He ever.

There was a wonderful woman in our city that grew up in the Shady Grove community north of Conway by the name of Janis Mack, who had lost her husband, Ralph, the year after Viola passed away. They owned and operated Pickles Gap Village, a tourist attraction outside Conway. While Janis and I had known each other for several years and held each other in high esteem, little did I know she had been reading my column for a long time and clipping out many of them from our local newspaper.

As only He can, over the next few months God brought us together and she is a dream come true. We were married on September 8, 2015, and make each other very happy. Janis is beautiful, talented, and has over 40 years of business experience, which includes banking and owning her own real estate company, along with Pickles Gap Village. She also has written four cookbooks. Janis is really excited about helping to spread the bookcase project all across the United States of America. To be sure, she is a very special lady and I have dedicated this book to her.

END

CPSIA information can be obtained
at www.ICGtesting.com
Printed in the USA
FSHW02n0303020518
47516FS